American STR★AMLINE

BERNARD HARTLEY & PETER VINEY

DESTINATIONS

An intensive American English course
for advanced students

Student's Edition

*American adaptation by Flamm/Northam Authors
and Publishers Services, Inc.*

D1737557

Oxford University Press

1985

Oxford University Press
200 Madison Avenue New York, N.Y. 10016 USA
Walton Street Oxford OX2 6DP England
OXFORD is a trademark of Oxford University Press.
© B. Hartley, P. Viney,
and Oxford University Press, 1985
First published 1985
Printing (last digit): 10 9 8 7 6 5

Library of Congress Cataloging in Publication Data

Hartley, Bernard
American Streamline Destinations

"American adaptation by Flamm/Northam Authors
and Publishers Services, Inc."

ISBN 0-19-434120-8 (student's ed.)
ISBN 0-19-434121-6 (teacher's ed.)
ISBN 0-19-434124-0 (cassette)

Illustrations by:
Cover: Paul Thomas; Unit 2: Hilary Newby/Publish-
ers Graphics; Unit 3: Paddy Mounter; Unit 4: London
Art Technical Drawings, Ltd.; Unit 10: Llynne Busch-
man; Unit 11: Bonnie Dann; Units 12 and 13: Irene
Trivas/Publishers Graphics; Unit 20: Ken Cox; Unit
21: Paul Sample; Unit 22: Bonnie Dann; Unit 23:
Susanna Ray; Unit 25: Hilary Newby/Publishers Gra-
phics; Units 28 and 29: Richard Draper; Units 31 and
34: Paddy Mounter; Unit 36: Ellis Nadler; Unit 37:
Irene Trivas/Publishers Graphics; Unit 38: Bonnie
Dann; Unit 39: Ken Cox; Unit 44: Llynne Buschman;
Unit 45: Mike Vaughan; Unit 46: Richard Draper;
Unit 47: Bill Prosser; Unit 53: Llynne Buschman; Unit
62: Bonnie Dann; Unit 63: Paul Sample; Unit 65: Mike
Saunders; Unit 66: Ron Jobson; Unit 67: Paddy Moun-
ter; Units 68 and 71: Llynne Buschman; Unit 72: Paul
Sample; Unit 73: Leslie Dunlap/Publishers Graphics;
Unit 74: Llynne Buschman; Unit 80: Paul Sample.

Photographs by:
Units 1, 18, 27, 52 (man and baby), 59 (cab drivers):
Catherine Noren; Units 14, 15, 33 (collage), 41, 48
(bottom), 60 and 77 (background): Halley Ganges.
Unit 4: courtesy of Fiat; Unit 7: C. Vergara/Photo
Researchers; Unit 9: Camera Press; Unit 16: John
Topham Picture Library; Unit 19: P and PF James;
Unit 32: UPI/Bettmann; Unit 33: published with per-
mission of The Dallas Morning News; Copyright ©
1980 by The New York Times Company. Reprinted by
permission; Reprinted with permission of the Village
Voice © 1980; Reprinted by permission of New York
News Inc. © 1980 New York News Inc. © News
Group Chicago, Inc., 1980 Reprinted with permission
of the Chicago Sun-Times; Reprinted by permission of
the San Francisco Examiner; Reprinted by permission of
the Miami Herald; Unit 40: left-hand page: (cable
car) Image Bank; (Las Vegas and Grand Canyon and
Minnie Mouse) Alan Hutchinson; right-hand page:
(background and bottom left) Image Bank; (top left
and middle) Colorific; Unit 41: Reprint by permission
of Nissin Foods(USA)Co.,Inc.; Unit 42: Terry Williams;
Unit 48: (top) Keyston Press Agency Ltd.; Unit 51:
(top) Metropolitan Home Magazine © Meredith
Corporation 1984. All rights reserved; (bottom) Eliza-
beth Whiting and Associates; Unit 52: (Debra Harry,
Telly Savalas) Syndication International; (Lauren
Bacall) Rex Features; Unit 56: Sunday Times; Unit 57:
The Kobal Collection; Unit 59: (bottom) Karen
Wollman; Unit 66: (satellite) Elizabeth Photo Library;
(Saturn) Sunday Times/NASA; (plaque and earth)
Space Frontiers; Unit 69: Tom McHugh/Photo Re-
searchers; Unit 70: BBC Hulton Picture Library;
Western Americana Picture Library; Unit 78: Jean
Photographs.

*The publishers would also like to thank the following
for their time and assistance:*

All-City Appliance	Gordon Fraser Gallery
Bell & Howell	Hallmark Cards, Inc.
Eastern Airlines	McDonald's Corporation
Goodyear Tire and	
Rubber Company	

Printed in Hong Kong

CONTENTS

ARRIVALS

Unit 1

A: Excuse me. Dolores Cotten?
B: Yes?
A: Hi. I'm Brad Jordan, from Orange Computers. How do you do?
B: How do you do? I'm glad to meet you, Brad. Thank you for coming to meet us.
A: It's a pleasure. How was the trip?
B: It was fine, thanks. Oh, I'd like you to meet Ron Eng. He's our sales manager.
A: How do you do, Ron?

Exercise 1

A: Bob Crawford?
B: . . .
A: Hello. I'm Helen Kirby, from General Technologies. How do you do?
B: . . .
A: It's a pleasure. Did you have a good trip?
B: . . .
A: Oh, let me introduce you to Charlie Vitto. He's our financial manager.
B: . . .

C: Karen!
D: Hi, Jody. How are you doing?
C: Just fine. How are you? I haven't seen you for ages.
D: I'm all right. Are you here to meet somebody?
C: No, my mother just left for Miami.
D: Do you have time for coffee?
C: Sure. I'd love a cup.

E: Margaret, hi.
F: Hello, Carol. How are you?
E: Oh, I'm O.K. How are you getting along?
F: Fine, thanks. How are Larry and the kids?
E: Everybody's fine. My car's just outside. Let me take one of your bags.
F: Oh, thanks. Careful, it's heavy.

G: Hi. What time is your next flight to New York?
H: 2:45. Flight 604 to Kennedy Airport. There is space available.
G: What's the fare—one way?
H: It's $56.70 with the tax.
G: O.K. Here you are. Put it on my Diners Club card, please.
H: All right. Just a second.

Exercise 2

Look at the conversation between G and H, and practice two similar conversations, one for New York and one for Chicago.

Streamline Air Departures from Middleburg		
Service to	**Flight**	**Departs**
New York		
(La Guardia)	317	11:05
New York (JFK)	604	2:45
Los Angeles	410	4:15
Chicago (O'Hare)	104	3:55
Atlanta	211	10:20

I: Well, hi there!
J: Uh—hello.
I: How are you doing?
J: Oh—fine. Uh—excuse me . . . do I know you from somewhere?
I: Sure, it's me, Rick Ballestrina.
J: I'm sorry. I don't think I know you.
I: Aren't you Jose Cortes?
J: No, I'm afraid not.
I: Oh, forgive me. I thought you were someone else. I'm so sorry.
J: That's all right.

Exercise 3

Listen to the airport announcements. Look at the example and complete the chart in the same way.

Airline	Flight	To	Gate	Departs
1. Streamline	604	New York (JFK)	3	2:45
2.				
3.				
4.				
5.				

Exercise 4

How are you?
I'm fine, thanks. How are you?
1. Hi!
2. I'm so sorry.
3. Thank you very much for helping me.
4. Aren't you Michael Jackson?
5. How are you getting along?
6. Here you are.
7. Excuse me.
8. Good-bye.

Streamline Air Fares (tax included)			
From Middleburg	**Mon-Thurs**	**Week-ends**	***Super Saver**
To New York			
one way	$56.70	$76.70	—
round trip	$113.40	$153.40	$89.00
To Chicago			
one way	$47.30	$65.30	—
round trip	$94.60	$130.60	$79.00

* Make reservation & buy ticket 2 weeks ahead.

IS EVERYTHING READY?

RALPH & EDWARD PRODUCTIONS

Program: This Is Your Life
Date: Nov. 3
Origin: KRKR, Los Angeles
Studio: 4
Subject: William Paine
Host: Joe Campanaro
Director: Chris Price

Running order

Pre-show
7:00 Admit studio audience.
7:30 Warm up (Comedian tells jokes to audience).
7:55 Limousine arrives (7-minute walk to studio).

Show
8:00 Start titles, music, commercial (Fizz).
8:01 Campanaro introduces show.
8:02 Paine arrives. Campanaro greets him.

Guests
8:03 Paine's sister from Japan.
8:05 His schoolteacher.
8:08 Commercials (Dr. Peppy & Daft Cheese).
8:09 Rita Colon, actress.
8:11 Mother.
8:12 Father.
8:14 John Galveston, movie director.
8:16 Commercials (Fizz & Daft Mayonnaise).
8:18 His first girlfriend.
8:19 Steve Newman, actor (his best friend).
8:21 Donna Parrot, Hollywood reporter.
8:23 Clips from Paine's latest movie.
8:27 His brother.
8:28 Commercials (Dr. Peppy & Alarmin Tissue).
8:29 Show ends. Start credits and music.

Post-show
8:30-8:45 Studio audience leaves.
8:45 Champagne party for Paine and guests.

"This Is Your Life" used to be one of the most popular programs on American television. Recently one of the national networks started the program again—not reruns but all-new shows. Every week a well-known person is invited to a TV studio, without knowing that he or she will be the subject of the program. The host greets the person with "This Is Your Life!" The person then meets friends and relatives from his or her past and present. The program is taped before a live audience. The taping begins at 8:00. It's 6:45 now and the director is checking the preparations with her new production assistant. The subject of tonight's show will be an actor, William Paine. The host, as usual, will be Joe Campanaro.

Director: Let's check the arrangements. We're bringing Bill Paine here in a rented limousine. He thinks he's coming to tape a talk show appearance. The driver has been told to arrive at exactly 7:55. The program begins at 8:00. At that time Bill will be walking to the studio. Joe will start his introduction at 8:01, and Bill will get here at 8:02. Joe will meet him at the door. Camera 4 will be there. Then he'll take him to that sofa. It'll be on Camera 3. Bill will be sitting there during the whole program. For most of the show Joe will be sitting next to the sofa or standing on that "X." He'll be on Camera 2. The guests will come through that door, talk to Bill and Joe, and then go backstage.

Director: Now, is that clear?
Production Assistant: Yes, but—uh—there is one thing.
Director: Well, what is it?
PA: Who's going to take care of the guests before they come on?
Director: Stephanie is.
PA: And where will they be waiting?
Director: In Room 401 we have a guest lounge. Stephanie will be sitting there with them. They'll be watching the show on a monitor. She'll cue them two minutes before they come on.
PA: O.K. I think that covers everything.

Exercise 1
Each of the guests will say a few words about William Paine.
A: *Who'll be speaking at 8:06?*
B: *His school teacher will.*
Ask and answer about: 8:04, 8:10, 8:15, 8:19, and 8:27.

Exercise 2
A: *What'll be happening at 7:45?*
B: *A comedian will be telling jokes to the audience.*
Ask and answer about: 7:57, 8:35, and 9:00.

Exercise 3
The guests will be waiting in Room 401 from 7:50 until they go on.
A: *How long will his sister be waiting?*
B: *She'll be waiting for thirteen minutes.*
Ask and answer about the other guests.

THIS IS YOUR LIFE!

Campanaro: Good evening and welcome to "This Is Your Life." I'm your host, Joe Campanaro. We're waiting for the subject of tonight's program. He's one of the world's leading actors, and he thinks he's coming here for a talk show. I think I hear him now ... Yes, here he is! William Paine, this is your life!

Paine: Oh, no! I can't believe it! Not me ...

Campanaro: Yes, you! Come in with me now. Ladies and gentlemen, William Paine! (Applause.) Sit right over here, Bill. Let's begin at the beginning. You were born in Providence, Rhode Island on July 2, 1942. You were the youngest of six children. Your mother was a model, and your father worked at a furniture store. Of course, your name was Herman Wartski then.

Campanaro: Do you recognize this voice?

Voice: I remember Herm—Bill—when he was two. He used to cry and scream all day.

Paine: Rosanne!

Campanaro: Yes, all the way from Tokyo—we flew her here to be with you tonight—your sister, Rosanne Wartski Tatsukawa.

Paine: Rosie, why didn't you tell me?

Campanaro: Yes, you haven't seen each other for 9 years. Take a seat next to him, Rosanne. You went to school in Providence and got your diploma from Whitney High School in 1960.

Campanaro: Do you remember this voice?

Voice: Herman! Stop daydreaming! I asked you a question!

Paine: Incredible! It's Mr. Theissen.

Campanaro: Your English teacher, Mr. Irwin Theissen. Was Bill a good student, Mr. Theissen?

Theissen: Well, not really. No, he was the worst in the class. But he was a great actor, even in those days. He could imitate all the teachers.

Campanaro: Thank you, Mr. Theissen. You can talk to Bill later. Well, you went on to the Yale School of Drama in 1962 and finished in 1966. In 1970 you went to Hollywood.

Campanaro: Do you know this voice?

Voice: Say, Bill, can you ride a horse yet?

Paine: Rita!

Campanaro: Yes, Rita Colon, who's flown in from New York, where she's appearing in the musical *34th Street.*

Colon: Bill, darling! It's so wonderful to see you. Hello, Joe, darling. Bill and I were in a movie together in 1974. Bill had to learn to ride a horse, and ... well, Bill doesn't like horses very much.

Paine: Like them? I'm scared to death of them!

Colon: Anyway, poor Bill practiced for 2 weeks. Then he went to the

director—it was John Galveston—and said, "What do you want me to do?" John said, "I want you to fall off the horse." Bill was furious. He said, "What?! Fall off?! I've been practicing for two weeks. I could fall off the first day—without any practice!"

Look at this:

Ralph & Edward Productions

Program: *This Is Your Life*
Date: *Nov. 3*
Origin: *KRKR, Los Angeles*
Studio: *4*
Subject: *William Paine*
Host: *Joe Campanaro*
Director: *Chris Price*

Subject's Biographical Data

Last name: *Wartski (stage name)*
First name: *Herman (William Paine)*
Middle name/initial: *I.*
Date of birth: *7/2/42*
Place of birth: *Providence, R.I.*
Nationality: *American (U.S.)*
Education: *Whitney H.S. Providence*
Yale School of Drama

Address: *77 Sunshine Boulevard*
Hollywood, CA.

Marital status: *Single*
Occupation: *Actor*

Ralph & Edward Productions

Program:
Date:
Origin:
Studio:
Subject:
Host:
Director:

Subject's Biographical Data

Last name:
First name:
Middle name/initial:
Date of birth:
Place of birth:
Nationality:
Education:

Address:

Marital status:
Occupation:

Ask questions and fill out the form for another student.

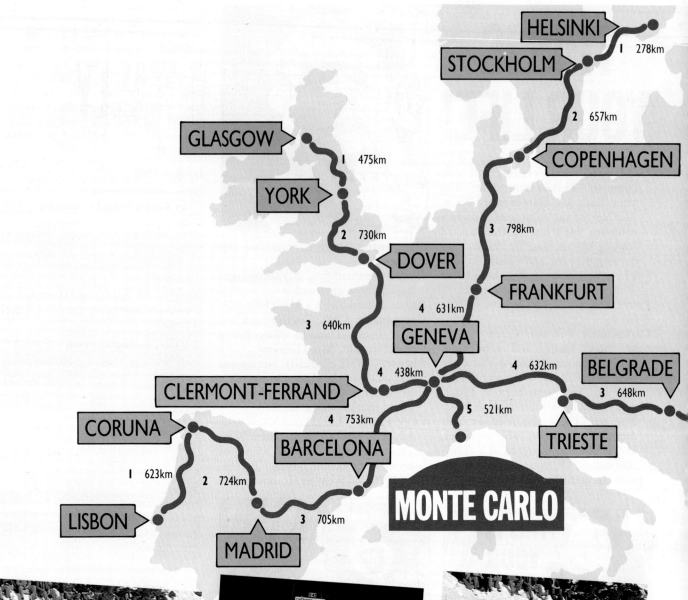

HELSINKI
278km

STOCKHOLM
1

2 657km

GLASGOW
1 475km

YORK

COPENHAGEN

2 730km

3 798km

DOVER

FRANKFURT

4 631km

3 640km

GENEVA

CLERMONT-FERRAND
4 438km

4 632km

BELGRADE

3 648km

CORUNA
5 521km

TRIESTE

1 623km
4 753km

2 724km

BARCELONA

MONTE CARLO

LISBON
3 705km

MADRID

Driver: Russell Cook
Nationality: British Age: 28
Starting point: Glasgow
Car: Talbot Sunbeam Lotus
Engine displacement: 132 cu. in
   (2172cc)
Top speed: 122 mph
Fuel economy: city 18 mpg, highway
   22 mpg
Overall dimensions
   Length: 150.4 in (382 cm)
   Width: 63 in (160 cm)
   Height: 54.7 in (139 cm)

Driver: Hannu Larsen
Nationality: Finnish Age: 32
Starting point: Helsinki
Car: Audi Quattro
Engine displacement: 131 cu. in (2144
   cc)
Top speed: 137 mph
Fuel economy: city 18 mpg, highway
   35 mpg
Overall dimensions
   Length: 173 in (440 cm)
   Width: 67.7 in (172 cm)
   Height: 52.8 in (134 cm)

Driver: Danielle Bernard
Nationality: French Age: 31
Starting point: Lisbon
Car: Renault 5 Gordini
Engine displacement: 85.2 cu. in
   (1397cc)
Top speed: 115 mph
Fuel economy: city 31 mpg, highway
   45 mpg
Overall dimensions
   Length: 137.8 in (350 cm)
   Width: 59.8 in (152 cm)
   Height: 54.7 in (139 cm)

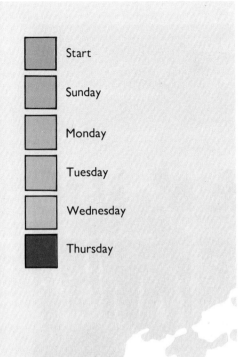

	Start
	Sunday
	Monday
	Tuesday
	Wednesday
	Thursday

2 703km

THESSALONIKI

1 543km

ATHENS

Driver: Sandro Rossi
Nationality: Italian   *Age:* 30
Starting point: Athens
Car: Fiat 131
Engine displacement: 97 cu. in
   (1585cc)
Top speed: 104 mph
Fuel economy: city 27 mpg, highway
   38 mpg
Overall dimensions
   Length: 167.7 in (426 cm)
   Width: 65 in (165 cm)
   Height: 54.7 in (139 cm)

THE MONTE CARLO RALLY

The Monte Carlo Rally, which started in 1911, is Europe's most famous car event. Competitors leave from several points around Europe and follow routes of approximately equal length to a rallying point which will be Geneva this year. Then they follow a single route to the finish. The rally consists of five daily stages, beginning on Sunday morning, and each competitor will have driven about 2000 miles by Thursday night. It is not a race. The winner is decided on a points system. Drivers have to maintain an average speed between control points, and there are also special tests of driving skill in different conditions on the way.

Rally News from CSN, Cable Sports Network

Now here's a report from Howard Sokell in England.

Hello from Dover. It's 9 o'clock on Monday, January 25th, and the British competitors in the Monte Carlo Rally have just arrived here at the end of the second stage in this year's contest. Russell Cook, who's driving a Sunbeam Lotus, is in the lead. The Triumph, driven by Tony Bond, who won last year's rally, crashed in Yorkshire this morning. Tony was not hurt, but he will be unable to continue. Seven other cars have withdrawn due to bad weather conditions. Tonight the cars, which left from Glasgow on Sunday morning, will be crossing the English Channel.

Exercise 1
Look at the first driver.
What's his name?
His name's Russell Cook.
Where does he come from?
He comes from Britain.
How old is he? He's 28.
Ask and answer questions about the other drivers.

Exercise 2
Look at the first car. (All statistics are for production cars.)
What make is it? It's a Sunbeam Lotus.

How fast can it go? The top speed is 122 mph.
How much gas does it use? 18 mpg in the city, 22 mpg on the highway.
How long is it? 150.4 in.
How wide is it? 63 in.
How high is it? It's 54.7 in.
Ask and answer questions about the other cars.

Exercise 3
Look at the drivers and the cars.
Danielle Bernard's older than Sandro Rossi.
Russell Cook isn't as old as Danielle Bernard.
Hannu Larsen's the oldest.
Make comparisons about the cars using: fast/long/wide/high/economical.

Exercise 4
Look at the first driver. All the cars started on Sunday morning.
Where is he now? He's in Dover.
Where did he start? He started in Glasgow.
How long has he been driving? He's been driving for two days.
How many miles has he driven? 748 miles.
Ask and answer questions about the other drivers.

Exercise 5
Look at the first driver. It's Monday night.
Where will he be tomorrow night?
He'll be in Clermont-Ferrand.
What will he be doing tomorrow?
He'll be driving from Dover to Clermont-Ferrand.
Ask and answer questions about Wednesday and Thursday.
Do the same for the other drivers.

Exercise 6
Look at the first driver.
On Tuesday night he'll be in Clermont-Ferrand.
How far will he have driven on Tuesday? He'll have driven 397 miles.
Ask and answer questions about Wednesday and Thursday.
Do the same for the other drivers.

OUT OF WORK

In the United States a lot of people are out of work. Tracy Kowalski is 19. She dropped out of high school two years ago and got a job as a check-out clerk in a supermarket. She was fired four months ago and hasn't been able to find another job yet.

"My old man just doesn't understand. He started working in the steel mill here in town when he was 16. Things are different now, but he thinks I should start bringing home some money. I'm on unemployment, but it isn't very much and I'm just fed up with standing in line to sign for it every other week. I hate having to ask my folks for money. My mom gives me a couple of dollars now and then, but she can't stand having me around the house all day. I've almost given up looking for a job. I look at the paper every day, but I'm really tired of going through the want ads. There are at least fifty people for every job. I was interested in becoming a receptionist for a dentist or a doctor because I like meeting people, but now I'd take any job that came along. People ask me why I don't move to California or maybe Houston, but I really don't want to leave my family and my friends. Anyway, I'd be scared of living all alone in a strange place."

Tracy went to the state employment office. She had to fill out a questionnaire. Here is part of it:

QUESTIONNAIRE

1. Do you want (check one)
   (a) full-time employment ☐
   (b) part-time employment ☐
2. What is most important for you?
   (Number these from 1 to 5 in order of importance — 1 = most, 5 = least)
   (a) money ☐ (b) people ☐
   (c) job security ☐ (d) job satisfaction ☐
   (e) interesting job ☐
3. Do you like (check "yes" or "no")

	yes	no
(a) meeting people?	☐	☐
(b) working alone?	☐	☐
(c) working with other people?	☐	☐
(d) working with your hands?	☐	☐
(e) traveling?	☐	☐
(f) working outdoors?	☐	☐

4. What do you do in your free time?
   (check "often", "sometimes", or "never")

George Hartman is 54. Until last year he was a foreman at an automobile plant in Michigan. He had worked for the same company since he graduated from high school. He had a good job and a comfortable life. When the company cut back production last year, George was laid off.

"It's funny, you know. I don't feel old, but it isn't easy to start looking for a job at my age. I've been turned down so many times that now I'm afraid of applying for a job. All the interviewers are twenty years younger than me. You see, I'm interested in learning a new skill, but nobody wants to train me. I can see their point of view, you know. I'll have to retire in a few years. It's just that . . . well, I'm tired of sitting around the house. I've worked hard for over thirty-five years, and now I'm terrified of having nothing to do. When I was still with U.S. Motors I was bored with doing the same thing day after day, but now I'd enjoy having a job again—any job. It's not just the money. I'm still on unemployment, and my wife has a good job. She makes more money than I ever did, but we have to be careful with expenses, and so I've given up smoking. But we're getting along. No, it's not just the money. I need to get out more and feel . . . useful, you know. Yeah, I guess I want to feel useful."

Exercise 1
I like meeting people.
Make sentences about yourself with: love/enjoy/like/don't like/dislike/hate/can't stand.

Exercise 2
I'm scared of living all alone.
Make sentences about yourself with: afraid of/terrified of/scared of.

Exercise 3
I'm bored with doing the same things.
Make sentences about yourself with: fed up with/bored with/tired of/interested in.

Exercise 4
I gave up smoking.
Make sentences about yourself with: start/begin/stop/give up.

GETTING A JOB

In the United States every state has an employment service which helps unemployed people who are looking for jobs. The local offices list job openings in the area, and give practical advice on interview techniques, application forms, letters, unemployment insurance, and Social Security. Young people, especially those without a college education, need to have this advice. Here is part of a brochure put out by one state.

THE INTERVIEW

So you're going to have an interview for a job. Great! Now for the hard part. To do well on an interview you need to give it some thought first. Employers want to learn if you are the person they want, so you'll be asked a lot about yourself. Think about it now, and you'll be able to give clear answers:

What do I do well? School activities?
What are my good points? School subjects?
Why would I like this job? Previous job?
Spare-time interests? Part-time work?
What is my family like?

What do I like doing and why?
What do I not like doing and why?

You will want to ask questions too:
The job itself? Can I see
Training? *Promotion* where I
Prospects for advancement? would be
Educational opportunities? working?
Conditions? Hours?
  $$$?
  money

Write down your answers and go over them just before you go into the interview.

BEFORE THE INTERVIEW

1. Find out all you can about the company.
2. Find out the interviewer's name and office phone number.
3. Find out where the interview is.
4. Find out how to get there and how long it will take you to get there.
5. Make sure you know what the job involves.
6. Dress to look clean and neat.

AT THE INTERVIEW

DOs
1. Arrive early. Call ahead if you're delayed.
2. Try to smile and show confidence.
3. Ask questions and show interest in the job.
4. Be polite, listen carefully, and speak clearly.
DON'Ts
1. Don't panic, even if faced by more than one person. (Breathe deeply and remember all your good points.)
2. Don't slouch or look bored. (Stand and sit straight; make eye contact.)
3. Don't smoke or chew gum.
4. Don't give one-word answers or say you don't care what you do.

Look at these ads for job openings.

Computer Operator
Experienced assistant IBM System 34. Duties: billing and inventory. Send resume or letter stating qualifications to: American Diversified, 485 5th Avenue, Beaver Falls, PA 15010. Equal Opportunity Employer M/F
  male/female

Dental Receptionist/Secretary
Part-time. Bilingual Spanish/English. Mature, bright. Respond with qualifications and salary requirements. Larkin Agency, 254 23rd Street, Pittsburgh, PA 15260.

Matsuda of Tokyo
Opportunities available for salesperson in Philadelphia boutique. Send resume with salary requirement and references to Nicole, 109 Broad St., Philadelphia, PA 19105.

A letter of application

1. Remember that the first impression is very important.
2. Type the letter neatly on good stationery.
3. Check for spelling mistakes. Use a dictionary if you are not sure of a word. Retype the letter if necessary.

4. Describe yourself, your qualifications, and your experience clearly.
5. If the ad tells you to write for an application form you do not need to give detailed information in your letter.
6. Follow standard business letter format. Address the letter and envelope clearly.

421 Lafayette Drive, Apt. 317
St. Paul, Minnesota 55105
April 4, 1984

Personnel Department
Continental Computer Corp.
935 Watson Ave.
St. Paul, MN 55101

Dear Sir or Madam:

In reference to your ad in today's *Standard*, I am interested in the opening for a trainee computer programmer. Please send me an application form and any further details. Thank you for your attention in this matter.

Yours truly,

Ashley Wychulis

Ashley Wychulis

BATTLE OF SHERIDAN STREET

By MARVIN ROTHSTEIN

Police and Housing Authority officials had to turn back again yesterday when they tried to talk to Mrs. Florence Hamilton. They estimated that at least twenty of Mrs. Hamilton's dogs (the exact number of dogs living with Mrs. Hamilton is not known) guarded both the front and back doors of her house at 875 Sheridan Street in the city's East Side section.

The city officials were hoping to speak to the 83-year old widow, who is still refusing to leave her home. Every other house in an area of several city blocks around Mrs. Hamilton's house has been demolished.

The Housing Authority plans to build a low-income housing project in the area. All of the other residents agreed to move when the Authority offered to relocate them to new apartments in the Hillside section.

Police wanted to use stronger methods to remove Mrs. Hamilton and her dogs from their house, but public opinion has forced them to take a more cautious approach.

continued on page B3

Channel 7 Newsdesk

Remember the lady and her dogs on Sheridan Street? We promised to follow the story, and tonight we have two reports. First, Alan Nelson at City Hall.

Report 1

Alan: The City Housing Authority isn't working on anything except the "Battle of Sheridan Street." It's one lady and her pets versus City Hall, and so far she's winning. I have here Ms. Hilda Martinez, the Director of the Housing Authority who has agreed to talk to us. Ms. Martinez, has the situation changed since yesterday?

Martinez: No, Alan, it hasn't. Mrs. Hamilton is still in her house, and she still refuses to talk to us.

Alan: What are you going to do?

Martinez: It's a touchy situation. We'd like her to come out peacefully. The police don't intend to arrest her, but she's a very stubborn lady!

Alan: Stubborn? Well, it is her home.

Martinez: Yes, and it's been her home for a long time, I know. But nobody else refused to move. You see, we're going to build 400 apartments in that area. We expect to have about 1200 people living there when the project is finished. You have to balance that against one person and a pack of dogs.

Alan: But Mrs. Hamilton was born in that house, and she tries to give a home to the poor homeless dogs of this city.

Martinez: Of course. But we have promised to relocate her and one of her dogs to a modern apartment in a senior citizens project. The other dogs will go to the ASPCA.

Alan: So, what happens next?

Martinez: We can't wait forever. We want the ASPCA to take all the dogs first. Then we hope to talk to Mrs. Hamilton and convince her to move. We have to do something soon.

Alan: This has been Alan Nelson for Channel 7 Newsdesk.

Report 2

Cindy Wong: I'm standing in front of the only house still occupied on the 800 block of Sheridan Street. We have managed to set up an interview with Mrs. Florence Hamilton, the occupant of the house. She has decided to speak to us, but she has demanded to see me alone except for a camera crew of two.

Cindy: Mrs. Hamilton, our viewers would like to hear your side of the story.

Hamilton: There's not much to say. They want me to move. I was born here, and I intend to die here. It's as simple as that. Down, Caesar! Sit! Cleo! Sit!

Cindy: But the Housing Authority really needs to have this land, and they have arranged to relocate you.

Hamilton: I know. But I can't take all my dogs, just one. I love them all, and I need to have company. They're all I have. Come back, Calpurnia! Sit! Sit!

Cindy: How long can you hold out here?

Hamilton: Oh, I have plenty of food. People bring me dog food. The city has threatened to cut off my water and lights, but I'll be all right.

Cindy: Thank you, Mrs. Hamilton.

Hamilton: You can tell the city for me that I want a house where I can keep my dogs, not a *(bleep)* apartment for *(bleep)* senior citizens!

Cindy: Uh, yes—uh, this has been Cindy Wong talking to Mrs. Florence Hamilton, who is fighting to keep her home and pets, for Channel 7 Newsdesk.

Exercise

" . . . the other residents **agreed to move** . . ." *Agreed to move* is verb + *to* + verb.

Read the page again and pick out the other examples of verbs with *to* and another verb.

SENDING A CARD

Greeting cards are big business in the United States. Millions of cards are sent every year, and you can buy cards for every special occasion—or for no particular occasion at all. You can send cards for Christmas, New Year's, Easter, birthdays, engagements, weddings, funerals, Valentine's Day, Mother's Day, Father's Day, Thanksgiving, Halloween, sickness, graduation, promotion, or just friendship.

Dear Linda & Max —
Congratulations!
Congratulations!
We were delighted to hear about the twins! Double the happiness — and double the work! We're willing to help at any time. Hope to see you all soon.
Best Wishes,
Alice & Doyle

TWINS! How Wonderful!

Sandy,
You now hold the key to the world!
Happy Sweet Sixteen!
Now my girl's Sweet Sixteen — a magical birthday. It's great to be young and have your whole life ahead of you.
Love, Uncle Dave

Dear Patsy:
Best Wishes on your Wedding
I was so happy to hear about your engagement. I'm sorry to miss the happy event. I wish I could be there. I'm anxious to hear all the details of your wedding and honeymoon.
All the best,
Deb

Dixie Lee & Beau,
Congratulations on your Silver Wedding Anniversary
Twenty-five years together! Neither of you look old enough to have a 25th anniversary. We're so happy for you and feel so lucky to have you as neighbors.
Gloria & Julio

With Sincere Sympathy
Jim —
I was so sorry to hear about your dad's passing. It's difficult to put into words how much he meant to me. I remember when he was our Little League coach. He was always ready to help me develop my abilities. I'm sorry I was unable to come to the funeral. Please express my condolences to your family. Reggie

25

Plan of Hospital
You are here

Dear Martha,
Get Well Soon
I was very upset to hear about your accident. I'll come to see you as soon as you can have visitors. I've enclosed something funny to read to keep your spirits up. I hope you get better soon.
Love,
Rachel

MARION COUNTY GAZETTE
MARCH 10
ANNOUNCEMENTS

BIRTHS Max and Linda (nee Blake) Hogg are the proud parents of darling twin girls, **Ima** and **Yura**, born on March 5 at the Lister Hill Hospital in Winfield.

WEDDINGS Patricia Anne McBride and William Joseph Grooms were married last Friday evening at the home of the bride's parents, **Mr. and Mrs. George F. McBride**, in Hamilton. **Mr. Grooms** is the son of **Mrs. Everett Slade** of Talapoosa and **Mr. John M. Grooms** of Lafayette. After a honeymoon in Puerto Rico "Patsy" and "Billy Joe" will make their home in Talapoosa.

BIRTHDAYS Sandra Klein celebrated her sixteenth birthday at a party given by her parents, **Midge and Bob Klein**, at the Harris Bowling Alley in Winfield on March 7.

ANNIVERSARIES Dixie Lee and Beau Pruitt were honored at a reception at the City Cafe in Lafayette to mark their Silver Wedding Anniversary on March 6. Their daughters **Sarah Alice (Flippo)**, **Connie Sue (Holcomb)**, and **Rita Mae** hosted the elegant party.

DEATHS James E. Seward died on March 8 at the Veteran's Hospital in Middleburg, aged 73. Survived by wife **Catherine**, son **James, Jr.**, daughter **Mary**, and five grandchildren. Services at Kilgore Funeral Home in Winfield on March 11 at 3:00 p.m. No flowers please. Memorial donations to American Heart Association.

ILLNESSES Martha (Mrs. Edward) Price is in Lister Hill Hospital, Room 235, in Winfield, with injuries resulting from a car accident. Her condition is serious, and she cannot have visitors yet.

Wedding anniversaries

The traditional gifts for each anniversary:

1st	paper	25th	silver
2nd	cotton	30th	pearl
3rd	leather	35th	jade
4th	linen	40th	ruby
5th	wood	45th	sapphire
10th	tin	50th	gold
15th	crystal	55th	emerald
20th	china	60th	diamond

Exercise
Can you suggest a suitable gift for each anniversary?
2nd anniversary
You could give a table cloth or some towels.

Unit

MARRIAGE COUNSELING

David and Barbara Weiner have been married for nearly fifteen years. They have two children, Gary, aged eleven, and Debbie, who is nine. During the last couple of years David and Barbara haven't been very happy. They argue all the time. Barbara's sister advised them to go to a marriage counselor. A marriage counselor helps married couples to talk about their problems and to solve them, if possible. Sometimes they meet the counselor separately, and other times they are together for the session. This is David and Barbara's third session with Dr. Joyce Sisters, the counselor.

Barbara's Interview

Dr. Sisters: Oh, come in, Barbara. Have a seat. Didn't David come?

Barbara: Yes, he's waiting outside. He didn't want to come here this week, but . . . well, I persuaded him to come.

Dr. Sisters: I see. How have things been going?

Barbara: Oh, about the same. We still seem to have fights all the time.

Dr. Sisters: What do you fight about?

Barbara: What don't we fight about? Oh, everything. You see, he's so inconsiderate . . .

Dr. Sisters: Go on.

Barbara: Well, I'll give you an example. You know, when the children started school, I wanted to go back to work again. So I got a job. Well, anyway, by the time I've picked Gary and Debbie up at school, I only get home about half an hour before David.

Dr. Sisters: Yes?

Barbara: Well, when he gets home, he expects me to run around and get dinner on the table. He never does anything in the house.

Dr. Sisters: Hmm.

Barbara: And last Friday! He invited three of his friends to come over for a drink. He didn't tell me to expect them, and I'd had a long hard day. I don't think that's right, do you?

Dr. Sisters: Barbara, I'm not here to pass judgement. I'm here to listen.

Barbara: I'm sorry. And he's so messy. He's worse than the kids. I always have to remind him to pick up his clothes. He just throws them on the floor. After all, I'm not his maid. I have my own career. Actually, I think that's part of the trouble. You see, I make more money than he does.

David's Interview

Dr. Sisters: David! I'm so glad you could come.

David: Hello, Dr. Sisters. Well, I'll be honest. Barbara had to force me to come, really.

Dr. Sisters: Does it embarrass you to talk about your problems?

David: Sure, it does. But I guess we need to talk to somebody.

Dr. Sisters: Barbara feels that you . . . well, that you resent her job.

David: I don't know. I'd like her to stay home, but she's very smart. So really, I encouraged her to go back to work. With the kids in school, she needs something to do. And I suppose we need the money.

Dr. Sisters: How do you share the housework?

David: I try to help. I always help her with the dishes, and I help Gary and Debbie to do their homework while she makes dinner. But she doesn't think that's enough. What do you think?

Dr. Sisters: I'm not here to give an opinion, David.

David: I think we're both too tired, that's all. In the evenings we're both too tired to talk. And Barbara . . . she never allows me to suggest anything about the house or about the kids. We always have the same arguments. She has her own opinions and that's it. Last night we had another fight. She's forbidden the kids to ride their bikes to school.

Dr. Sisters: Why?

David: She thinks they're too young to ride in the traffic. But I think they should. She always complains about picking them up at school. But they can't be tied to their mother's apron strings all their lives, can they?

Exercise 1
"Barbara's sister advised *them* to go . . ."
There are fifteen sentences like this. Underline them or write them out.

Exercise 2
They're very tired. They can't talk.
They're too tired to talk.
Continue.
1. They're very young. They shouldn't ride bikes to school.
2. He's very old. He can't go to work.
3. We were very surprised. We couldn't say anything.
4. She's very sick. She shouldn't go out.

Unit 9

A FUNNY THING HAPPENED TO ME...

A funny thing happened to me last Friday. I'd gone into Chicago to do some shopping. I wanted to get some Christmas presents, and I needed to find a book for my psych course (I'm a junior at Northwestern University in Evanston). I had gotten to the city early, so by early afternoon I'd bought everything that I wanted. Anyway, I'm not crazy about downtown Chicago—all the noise and traffic and strange people—and I'd made plans for that night. I just wanted to get in my car and drive home before the rush hour, but I felt really tired. I decided that I had time for a cup of coffee and a short rest. I bought a *Tribune* and went into a small cafeteria near the garage where I had parked my car. I got a cup of coffee and a package of doughnuts—glazed doughnuts. I'm crazy about glazed doughnuts. There were plenty of empty tables, and I found one near the window. I sat down and started the crossword puzzle in the paper. I always enjoy doing crossword puzzles.

A few minutes later a woman sat down across from me at my table. That surprised me because there were several empty tables. There was nothing strange about her except that she was very tall. In fact, she looked like a typical businesswoman—you know, conservative suit, briefcase—even a tie. I didn't say anything; I just kept doing the crossword. Suddenly she reached across the table, opened my package of doughnuts, took one out, dunked it in her coffee, and began to eat it. I couldn't believe my eyes! I was too shocked to say anything. Anyway, I didn't want to make a scene, so I decided to ignore it. I always avoid trouble if I can. I just took a doughnut myself and went back to my crossword.

When the woman took a second doughnut I didn't make a sound.

I pretended to be very interested in the puzzle. A few minutes later I casually put out my hand, took the last doughnut, and glanced at the woman. She was staring at me furiously. I nervously started eating the doughnut and decided to leave. I was ready to get up and go when the woman suddenly pushed back her chair, stood up, and hurried out of the cafeteria. I felt very relieved and decided to wait for two or three minutes before going myself. I finished my coffee, folded my newspaper, and stood up. And there, on the table, where my paper had been, was my package of doughnuts.

Look at this:

"I'd gone into Chicago to *do* some shopping."
"I always enjoy *doing* crossword puzzles."
"I didn't want to *make* a scene."
"I didn't *make* a sound."

Do	Make
shopping	a scene
work	plans
homework	an offer
housework	a suggestion
the cleaning	a decision
the dishes	a bed
gardening	an effort
something	an excuse
interesting	a mistake
a good job	a noise
business	a (phone) call
errands	a profit
a favor	dinner
a puzzle	trouble
	a list

Exercise

I always do my homework.
I made my bed this morning.
Write ten sentences, five with *do* and five with *make*.

POLITE REQUESTS

Benny Goldman used to be a popular comedian on American radio. He's nearly 70 now, but he still performs at hotels in the Catskill Mountains and other resorts in the Northeastern United States. He's on stage now at Borshsinger's Hotel in Monticello, a town in the Catskills.

Well, good evening, ladies and gentlemen—and others! It's nice to be back in Monticello at Borshsinger's again. I have to say that; I say it every night. I said it last night. The only trouble was that I was at Marco's Palace in Atlantic City. I thought the audience looked confused! Actually, I remember Monticello very well. Really! You know the first time I came here was in the 1930s. I was very young and very shy (Thank you, Mother). You can't believe that, can you? You can't imagine me either young or shy, but I was—very young and very shy. Anyway, the first Saturday night I was in Monticello I decided to go to a dance, but not at a fancy hotel like Borshsinger's. I told you I was very young and very shy. I forgot to add "very poor." Were any of you ever poor? Or young? Then maybe you remember the old Majestic Ballroom on Empire State Street. There's a parking lot there now. It was a wonderful place, always full of beautiful girls—the ballroom, not the parking lot. Of course, most of them are grandmothers now. Oh, were you there too, dear? I was too shy to ask anyone to dance. So I sat down at a table, and I thought I'd watch for a while—you know, see how the other guys did it. At the next table there was a pretty girl in a blue dress. She'd come in with a friend, but her friend was dancing with someone. Some dude came over to her, really spiffy-looking, wearing a blue suit and a fancy silk tie. Well, he walked over to her and said, "Excuse me. May I have the pleasure of the next dance?" She looked up at him (she had beautiful big blue eyes) and said, "Hmm? What did you say?" So he said, "I wonder if you would be kind enough to dance with me—uh—if you don't mind." "Oh. No, but thank you anyway," she replied.

A few minutes later this other turkey showed up. He had on a tweed sport coat and a bow tie and a little mustache. He gave her this big smile and said, "Would you please have the next dance with me?" "Pardon?" she said. I thought to myself, "She's a little deaf—or maybe she hasn't washed her ears recently."

"Would you mind having the next dance with me?" he said, a little nervously this time. "Oh. No thanks. I'm finishing my lemonade," she replied. "Wow!" I thought, "This looks really tough."

Then another fellow came over. He was very good looking—you know, wavy blonde teeth and bright white hair. Oops, I mean bright white teeth and wavy blonde hair. "May I ask you something?" he said very politely. "Certainly you may," she answered. "Can I—I mean, could I—uh—*may* I have the next dance with you?" "I'm sorry," she said. "My feet are killing me. I've been standing up all day at the store." By now, I was terrified. I mean she'd said no to all of them! Then this other character thought he'd give it a try.

"Would you like to dance?" he said. "What?" she replied. She was a very pretty girl, but I didn't think much of her voice! "Do you want to dance?" he said. She looked straight at him. "No," she said. That's all—"No." Well, I decided to go home. I was wearing an old jacket and an even older pair of pants, and nobody ever accused me of being good looking! Just as I was walking past her table, she smiled. "Uh—dance?" I said. "Thank you. I'd love to." she replied. And that was that! It's our forty-fifth anniversary next week.

Exercise 1
Go through and underline all the "requests." How many are there?

Exercise 2
There are six words that mean "man." What are they?

Exercise 3
Find the expressions that mean:
1. expensive and elaborate
2. a short time
3. appeared
4. unable to hear well
5. difficult, hard
6. handsome
7. make an attempt

A: Mike?
B: Yeah?
A: Close the door, will you? It's freezing in here.
B: Sure. I'm sorry.

shut the window/cold
open the door/very hot

C: Karen?
D: Hmm?
C: Lend me 50 cents. I left my purse in the office.
D: Oh, O.K. Here.
C: Thanks.

$5/wallet $1/handbag

E: Excuse me. Could you pass me the sugar?
F: Of course. There you are.
E: Thank you very much.

cream   salt   pepper

G: Do you need some help?
H: Oh, thank you. Would you mind putting my suitcase up on the rack?
G: Not at all. There you go.
H: Oh, thank you so much. You're very kind.

bag/under the seat
shopping bag/rack

I: Excuse me. It's stuffy in here. Do you mind if I open the window?
J: No, I don't mind at all. I'd like some fresh air too.

cold/close/cold too
feel hot/open/stuffy too

K: Excuse me, Lorraine. Could I ask you something?
L: Sure, Wendy. What is it?
K: Can I have the day off next Friday?
L: Well, we're very busy now. Is it important?
K: Yeah, it is, really. It's my cousin's wedding.
L: Oh, well, of course you can!

Tuesday/sister
Wednesday/nephew
Thursday/niece

M: Can I help you, ma'am?
N: I beg your pardon?
M: Can I help you, ma'am?
N: Oh. No, no thanks. I'm just looking.

Sir/Pardon?
Miss/Excuse me?

O: Good morning.
P: Good morning. I wonder if you can help me. I'm looking for a Christmas present for my father.
O: Have you thought about a nice tie?
P: Hmm . . . maybe. Could you show me some of your ties?

wedding/cousin/some towels
birthday/mother/scarf

Q: Excuse me.
R: Yes?
Q: I wonder if you'd mind handing me one of those cans of peas—on the top shelf. I can't reach it.
R: Oh, sure. There you are.
Q: Thank you very much.

box of cornflakes   package of pasta
roll of paper towels   bottle of oil

Unit 11

A TRIP TO LOS ANGELES

James Hall has a new job with Orange Computers in Philadelphia. He's 23 and just out of college. As part of his training he has to spend six weeks at company headquarters near Los Angeles. It's his first business trip, and he's packing his suitcase. He lives with his parents, and his mother is helping him.

Mrs. Hall: Jimmy, haven't you finished packing yet?

James: No, Mom, but it's all right. There isn't much to do.

Mrs. Hall: Well, I'll give you a hand. Oh. There isn't much room left. Is there anywhere to put your shaving kit?

James: Yeah, sure. It'll go in here. Now, I have three more shirts to pack. They'll go on top, but there's another pair of shoes to get in. I don't know where to put them.

Mrs. Hall: Put them here, one on each side. There. O.K. I think we can close it now.

James: O. K. Where's the tag?

Mrs. Hall: What tag, dear?

James: The name tag that the airline gave me to put on the suitcase. Oh, here it is.

Mrs. Hall: Now, do you have the key?

James: What key?

Mrs. Hall: The key to lock the suitcase, of course.

James: It's in the lock, Mom. Don't make such a production. There's nothing to worry about. There's plenty of time.

Mrs. Hall: Have you forgotten anything?

James: I hope not.

Mrs. Hall: And you have a safe pocket for your traveler's checks?

James: Yes, they're in my inside coat pocket.

Mrs. Hall: Do you have a book to read on the plane?

James: Yes, it's in my briefcase.

Mrs. Hall: What about small change to make phone calls?

James: Check. I have a pocketful of coins.

Mrs. Hall: And is everything all arranged?

James: What do you mean?

Mrs. Hall: Well, is there someone to meet you in Los Angeles?

James: No, Mom. I'll rent a car and go to a motel near the Orange office. They suggested the Newport Beach Holiday Inn.

Mrs. Hall: Do you have a reservation?

James: I hope so. I asked them to make it—the motel reservation, I mean. (I reserved the car myself.)

Mrs. Hall: Well, you've taken care of everything. I don't know why I'm worrying. Take care of yourself and be good. Call us tonight.

James: Thanks, Mom. I will.

Mrs. Hall: Oh, I nearly forgot! Here's some gum to chew on the plane—you know, when it's coming down. It's sugarless.

James: Oh, Mom. Don't worry. I'll be all right. I'll see you next month.

Exercise 1

James lives in Teaneck, New Jersey, across the Hudson River from New York City. His mother drove him to a bus stop in Teaneck. He took a bus to New York, then a subway train to Kennedy Airport, and finally a plane to Los Angeles. How can you get to your nearest airport? What is the best way for you to get there?

Exercise 2

James made a list. Look at it.
He remembered to pack his shirts.
He forgot to pack his raincoat.

Exercise 3

Think about the clothes you would pack for a two-week trip to New York or Boston in the spring. Imagine that you have just been on a plane and the airline has lost your suitcase. Make a list of the clothes you had in your suitcase.
one dark blue wool sweater
one brown leather belt

FLYING TO L.A.

At the airport

James is at the Pan American Terminal at Kennedy Airport. He's already checked in. He's been through the security check, and he's gone to the gate to wait for his flight. Listen to the announcements. Look at the screen, look at the example, and complete the chart in the same way.

PAN AM			
FLIGHT	**DESTINATION**	**GATE**	**DEPARTS**
932	Syracuse	14	3:25
217			
558			
563			
67			
811			

In flight

James is now on the plane. Listen to the announcements, and answer these questions.

1. What's the pilot's name?
   What are they waiting for?
   How long will the delay be?
   When will they arrive in Los Angeles?
2. What kind of plane is it?
   How fast is it going?
   Where is the plane?
   How hot is it in Los Angeles?
   What's the weather like?
   Why should the passengers keep their seat belts fastened?
3. What's the plane beginning to do?
   What should the passengers do?
   When can they start smoking again?
4. What should the passengers do?
   When can they stand up?
   Who should they see if they have questions?

Excuse me, young man. Would you mind opening the window? It's rather hot in here.

Dinner on the plane

Flight Attendant: Are you having dinner, sir?

James: Yeah—uh—yes, thanks.

Flight Attendant: We have a choice today of chicken or steak.

James: I'll take the steak. Could I get some red wine with that?

Flight Attendant: The beverage cart will come down this aisle in a few minutes. You can order your wine then.

James: Thank you. Is there a charge for the wine?

Flight Attendant: Yes. The soft drinks are free.

In flight questionnaire

Flight Attendant: Excuse me, sir. Would you mind filling out this questionnaire?

James: What's it about?

Flight Attendant: We want to learn more about our passengers so we can provide the best service.

James: Sure, I'll fill it out.

PAN AM PASSENGER QUESTIONNAIRE

Please take a few minutes to fill out this questionnaire and return it to your flight attendant. Thank you.

Date __/__/__   Flight No. _____

From _____   To _____

How many trips do you make in the U.S. in a year?

1 - 2 ☐   3 - 5 ☐   6 - 9 ☐   More ☐

Business ☐   Leisure ☐   Other _____

What cities do you travel to most frequently?

Chicago ☐   New York ☐   Los Angeles ☐

Houston ☐   Other _____

Why are you flying Pan Am today?

Best schedule ☐   Past experience ☐

Travel agent's recommendations ☐

Advertising ☐   Other _____

Auto rental

James: You have no record of my reservation? What do I do now?

Attendant: We have several cars, sir. Let's fill out this form. O.K. Hall, James. Address?

James: 427 Battle Terrace, Teaneck, New Jersey 07666

Attendant: Are you here on business or pleasure?

James: Business.

Attendant: How long will you need the car?

James: I don't know for sure. Put down two days. The company might pay for more.

Attendant: All right. Let me see your driver's license and a major credit card.

MONEY

Money is used for buying or selling goods, for measuring value and for storing wealth. Almost every society now has a money economy based on coins and paper bills of one kind or another. However, this has not always been true. In primitive societies a system of barter was used. Barter was a system of direct exchange of goods. Somebody could exchange a sheep, for example, for anything in the marketplace that they considered to be of equal value. Barter, however, was a very unsatisfactory system because people's precise needs seldom coincided. People needed a more practical system of exchange, and various money systems developed based on goods which the members of a society recognized as having value. Cattle, grain, teeth, shells, feathers, skulls, salt, elephant tusks, and tobacco have all been used. Precious metals gradually took over because, when made into coins, they were portable, durable, recognizable, and divisible into larger and smaller units of value.

A coin is a piece of metal, usually disc-shaped, which bears lettering, designs or numbers showing its value. Until the eighteenth and nineteenth centuries, coins were given monetary worth based on the exact amount of metal contained in them, but most modern coins are based on face value—the value that governments choose to give them, irrespective of the actual metal content. Coins have been made of gold (Au), silver (Ag), copper (Cu), aluminum (Al), nickel (Ni), lead (Pb), zinc (Zn), plastic and in China even from pressed tea leaves. Most governments now issue paper money in the form of bills, which are really "promises to pay." Paper money is obviously easier to handle and much more convenient in the modern world. Checks and credit cards are being used increasingly, and it is possible to imagine a world where "money" in the form of coins and paper currency will no longer be used. Even today, in the United States, many places, especially filling stations will not accept cash at night for security reasons.

Exercise 1
Find expressions which mean:
1. A place to buy gas
2. A place where goods are bought and sold
3. The period between 1801 and 1900
4. The bony structure of the head
5. Round and flat in shape
6. An exchange of goods for other goods

Exercise 2
Find words which mean:
1. Can be divided
2. Lasts a long time
3. Can be carried
4. Can be recognized

Exercise 3
Put these words in the correct places in the sentences below:
coins/cash/currency/money
1. The . . . of Japan is the yen.
2. She has a lot of . . . in her bank account.
3. It costs $20 if you're paying in . . . It'll be more if you pay by check.
4. Can you change this dollar bill into . . . for the coffee machine?

Exercise 4
Money is used for buying goods.
This sentence means: *You can buy goods with it.*
Write similar sentences which mean:
1. You can measure value with it.
2. You can store wealth with it.
3. You can sell things for it.

Exercise 5
Money is used for buying and selling goods.
People use money for buying and selling goods.
Change these sentences in the same way:
1. A system of barter was used.
2. Cattle, grain, and tobacco have all been used.
3. Paper currency will no longer be used.
4. Checks and credit cards are being used.

Exercise 6
Somebody could exchange a sheep.
A sheep could be exchanged.
Change these sentences in the same way:
1. People needed a more practical system.
2. Most governments now issue paper money in the form of bills.
3. Filling stations will not accept cash at night.

Exercise 7
Money *is used for buying things.*
Shampoo *is used for washing your hair.*
Make sentences with: knife/pen/key/camera/suitcase/toothpaste/detergent/wallet/hair dryer.

Exercise 8
A place where you can fill your gas tank is a *filling station.*
Complete these sentences:
1. A special room where you can wait is a . . .
2. A pill which helps you to sleep is a . . .
3. An account on which you can write checks is a . . .
4. A glove which boxers wear is a . . .
5. Oil you can cook with is . . .
6. A pool where you can swim is a . . .
7. Special liquid you can wash dishes with is . . .

MONEY, MONEY, MONEY

Bargaining

Sally Grooms is at a flea market in a small Pennsylvania town. She's just seen a glass bowl at one of the stands. She collects American glass objects made during the Depression of the 1930s. She's interested in buying the bowl. Listen to her conversation with the owner of the stand, and answer these questions.

1. How much does he say it's worth?
2. How much is he asking for it?
3. What does "buck" mean?
4. He suggests four different prices. Write them down.
5. She makes four offers. Write them down.

Some sayings in English about money:

Neither a borrower nor a lender be.

From Hamlet *by William Shakespeare.*

Have you ever borrowed money from anyone? Who from? How much?

Have you ever lent money to anyone? Who to? How much?

Are you in debt at the moment? (i.e., do you owe anyone any money?)

Does anyone owe you any money? Who? How much?

A penny saved is a penny earned.

Benjamin Franklin

Do you save money? Are you saving for anything at the moment? What?

Do you keep your money (a) in the bank? (b) in a safe? (c) in a book? (d) under the bed? (e) in the refrigerator?

Do you have a bank account? Do you have a checking account or a savings account? What's the interest rate? If your account was overdrawn, how much would the bank charge you?

Buy now; pay later.

Have you bought anything on credit? What? Did you pay a deposit? Do you think it's a good idea?

Do you have a credit card? Which one? (Visa? American Express? Diner's Club? Mastercard?)

When you pay cash, do you ask for a discount? Do you usually get it?

All progress is based upon a universal innate desire on the part of every organism to live beyond its income.

Samuel Butler

Do you spend more than you earn or less than you earn?

Do you have a budget for your money?

Do you keep a record of your expenses? Why?

A fool and his money are soon parted.

Where do you carry your spending money?
(a) in a purse (b) in a wallet (c) in a pocket

If you keep it in a pocket, which pocket do you keep it in?
(a) inside pocket of coat/jacket
(b) breast pocket of coat/jacket
(c) side pocket of coat/jacket
(d) back pocket of pants
(e) front pocket of pants

Have you ever had your pocket picked?

When you stay in a hotel, do you hide your money? Where?
(a) in your suitcase (b) under the mattress (c) in the pillow (d) in a book (e) somewhere else

Is gambling legal or illegal in your city/state/country? Do people bet? What do they bet on?
(a) cards (b) horse racing (c) dog racing (d) football/soccer/other sport (e) boxing (f) national lottery (g) something else

The customer is always right.

Have you bought anything this week? What?

What did it cost? Was it worth it?

Was it new or used?

Was it a bargain? Did you get a receipt?

Have you ever returned anything you had bought? What? Where?

Did you get your money back, a new article, a different article, or credit for a future purchase?

INSIDE STORY

"ECHO" REPORTER MISSING IN MANDANGAN WAR

PETTYVILLE, MANDANGA, May 12. Julie Mendoza, the veteran "Daily Echo" war correspondent, who is covering the civil war in Mandanga, has been reported missing.

Mendoza was last seen yesterday morning driving her jeep near the front line. The vehicle was found last night, but there was no sign of Mendoza. It is possible that she was ambushed and captured by rebel forces. Mendoza has been a war correspondent for many years and has covered a number of conflicts in different parts of the world. She has won two Pulitzer prizes for her

MENDOZA FREE

PETTYVILLE, MANDANGA, May 22. "Echo" war correspondent Julie Mendoza walked into a government forces camp this morning after spending ten days with Free Mandanga rebels. She appeared well and unharmed. She spoke to her brother and this paper by telephone before she was taken to her

IBC Evening News

The fighting between government and rebel forces in Mandanga continues tonight, with no end in sight. The only good news from that war-torn country was that war correspondent Julie Mendoza is alive and well. She was missing for ten days, but this morning she appeared at a government forces camp. We go to Pettyville for a report from Hank McLaughlin.

McLaughlin: Julie Mendoza is with me here at the Interhemisphere Hotel. After ten days with Mandangan rebels, she returned to Pettyville today. Julie, can you tell us how you were captured?

Mendoza: I was on my way to a vil-

lage near the front line. I came around a bend in the road, and there was a tree lying across the road. I managed to stop in time. Suddenly, armed men appeared on all sides!

McLaughlin: What did you do?

Mendoza: What would anybody do? I put my hands up! Anyway, they made me get out of my jeep; then they made me lie down on the ground. I thought, "This is it. They're going to shoot me!"

McLaughlin: What happened next?

Mendoza: Well, they searched me and the jeep. I didn't have any weapons, just a camera and a tape recorder. It's funny—they let me keep them. They tied my hands together and blindfolded me. Then they made me get in the back of a truck and lie under some sacks. I have no idea where they took me, except that it was a pretty big training camp. I was there for ten days.

McLaughlin: Were you treated well?

Mendoza: More or less. They let me walk around, and let me take pictures, but not of any of their faces. I was able to interview some of the leaders.

McLaughlin: How did you escape?

Mendoza: I didn't. They put me back

in the truck, blindfolded me again, drove for a few hours, then made me get out, and let me go.

McLaughlin: What exactly did the rebel leaders say?

Mendoza: I'll be writing about that for my readers first, Hank.

McLaughlin: Huh? Oh. Yes. This has been Hank McLaughlin reporting for IBC News in Mandanga.

MANDANGAN REBEL LEADERS PROMISE FIGHT TO DEATH

by JULIE MENDOZA

(This is the first of a three-part report written by Julie Mendoza, who spent 10 days with Mandangan rebels after her capture on May 11. The rebels forced her to go with them to their camp. However, they allowed her to keep her camera and tape recorder and to interview rebel leaders. Exclusive pictures on page 2.)

PETTYVILLE, MANDANGA, May 25. "We will fight till we win or die," declared

Exercise

When I was younger, my parents made me go to bed early.
When I was younger, my parents didn't let me go out at night.
Write true sentences about when you were younger.

PREFERENCES

A: What are you doing tomorrow night?
B: Nothing. Why?
A: Well, do you like country music?
B: Yes, I do—very much.
A: What do you like best—country western or bluegrass?
B: I like both, as a matter of fact.
A: Joe Ed Davis is playing at the Ale House. Would you like to go?
B: Yes, great! He's one of my favorites!

C: Hey, Charlene, look over here. They have a fabulous selection of designer jeans!
D: Oh, yeah! And they have my size!
C: But only Calvin Pines and Gloria Randibilts.
D: Yeah. Hmm. I don't like either one of them very much. I really wanted some Sergio Potentes.
C: But they don't have them in your size. Go ahead and try on a pair of Calvin Pines.
D: Nah. I'll wait and see if I find some Sergio Potentes somewhere else.

E: Well, have you decided yet? What do you want to see?
F: *A Moment of Peace* is on at the Arapahoe Two. I'd like to see that.
E: You would? I'd rather see *War in Space*.
F: Oh, no! The reviews were terrible.
E: I know, but it sounds like fun. *A Moment of Peace* is in French and I'd really rather not have to read subtitles.
F: Then how about *California Sunset*?
E: I'd rather not. I can't stand Steve Newman.
F: Well, you choose then.
E: Actually, I don't want to see any of them. I'd much rather stay home and watch TV.

G: What are you up for?
H: I don't know. There isn't much choice, is there?
G: No, not really. What would you rather have? Chicken a la King or spaghetti and meatballs?
H: I can't make up my mind. Uh—I'd just like a tuna fish sandwich.
G: We can look at the regular menu, if you'd like.
H: Nah, it's not worth it. I'll have the spaghetti.

This week in Denver

Jazz, Rock, Pop

★ **Blaze Foley** and **the Ramblers** (country and western) Billy's (861- 9540), Wed. & Thurs.

★ **Joe Ed Davis** and **the Harris County Line Band**, (bluegrass) Ale House (499-3773), Tues. — Thurs.

★ **Huey Lewis and the News** (Rock) Sharon Hall (861-4500), Fri. midnight

★ **Pat Benatar** in concert. Memorial Coliseum (499-5000), Sat. 8 p.m.

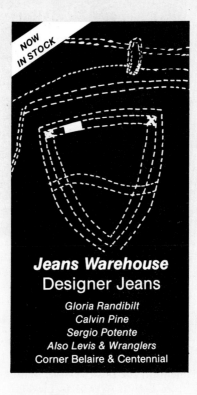

Jeans Warehouse
Designer Jeans

Gloria Randibilt
Calvin Pine
Sergio Potente
Also Levis & Wranglers
Corner Belaire & Centennial

Movies

Arapahoe 1 & 2
Halloween XII (PG)
A Moment of Peace (R) (Fr., Eng. subtitles)

Baronet
California Sunset (PG)
Steve Newman,
Gloria Gusto

Classic Cinema
Casablanca (no rating) Ingrid Bergman, Humphrey Bogart; and
Play It Again, Sam (G) Woody Allen

Paramount
War in Space (G) Raquel Evans, Chase Carson, Milly Thompson

Ritz
The Day We Had (R) Muriel Street, Jeremy Steel

TONIGHT'S TOPIC: 42ND STREET

"Good evening. I'm Harry Barber and this is Radio Station WLFM. Our topic tonight on 'Call In' is New York's 42nd Street, particularly the Times Square area. It's the most crime-filled area in the city. It's a place for drug dealers and alcoholics, action movies and pornography. It's inhabited by all kinds of street people from bag ladies and homeless kids to street corner orators and junkies. And it's becoming more and more dangerous. What should the city do? What do you listeners think? Call in. Maybe you can suggest some solutions."

"Hi, Harry. My name's Stuart Amos. I think the city should spend time doing something about it. They ought to redevelop the whole area. They ought to get rid of the pornography. I stopped going to that area a long time ago because I was really afraid that I'd get mugged or something. I mean, you never see a cop down there. And the Times Square subway station is full of strange characters. Somebody ought to do something. It's disgraceful."

"Thanks, Stuart, for your opinion. Now would someone call in and tell us what the city should do?"

"Hello, Harry. I'm Hilda Diaz. I agree with Mr. Amos. When I was young, I used to go to Times Square with my parents. But I wouldn't take my kids there now. There are too many bad influences like stores that specialize in pornography or weapons. And you always hear foul language in the street. Also it's the theater district. I love the theater even though it's so expensive. But I have to take public transportation to get there, and I won't risk my life taking the subway when I leave the theater at night. So I never go. Anyway, people have been talking about these problems for ten years and nothing has been done. We'd better not spend another minute talking about it. We'd better do something about it soon!"

"Right, Hilda. I'm sure we all sympathize with you. But lots of people think the city had better do something. Isn't there anyone who can offer a concrete solution? Call in, please."

"Harry, I'm Andrea Martin. I'd like to mention the positive side. 42nd Street from Eighth Avenue to Eleventh Avenue used to be just as bad—full of crumbling buildings and dirty, run-down fast food restaurants. In the past few years the city has redeveloped the area. It's become a new theater district. And it's not so expensive, so everyone can go to the theater there. There are also lovely restaurants and nice stores. We ought to give credit to the city for doing this."

"Thanks, Andrea. But don't you think the city ought to do more? O.K. Who's our next caller?"

"Harry, my name's Milton Kramer. I'm the chairman of the Committee to Redevelop 42nd Street. Obviously you haven't heard of this project, so I'll tell you and your listeners about it. In the next six years we plan to renovate the street's historic theaters, redesign the Times Square subway station, and build a 560-room hotel and four new office buildings. This will eliminate the lawless elements in the area and bring in theater-goers, office workers, and tourists. So you see, a solution already exists. And Harry, I think you'd better do your homework before you ask questions that already have answers."

Exercise

Find words which mean:
1. people who drink too much
2. public speakers
3. clearly
4. share the same feelings
5. falling apart
6. make over
7. take a chance
8. homeless woman who carries belongings in shopping bags
9. shameful
10. without a place to live

NIGHT FLIGHT

"This is your captain, John Cook speaking. Our estimated time of arrival in Anchorage is one a.m., so we've got a long flight ahead of us. I hope you enjoy it. Our flight attendants will be serving dinner shortly. Thank you."

It was Christmas Eve 1959, and the beginning of another routine flight. The flight attendants started preparing the food trays. A few of the passengers were trying to get some sleep, but most of them were reading. There was nothing to see from the windows except the vast blackness of the winter night. The plane was nearly full. A lot of the passengers were traveling home to spend Christmas with their families. The flight attendants started serving dinner.

It was a smooth and quiet flight. The flight attendants had finished picking up the trays, and they were in the galley putting things away when the first buzzers sounded. One of the flight attendants went along the aisle to check. When he came back he looked surprised. "It's amazing," he said. "Even on a smooth flight like this two people have been sick."

Twenty minutes later nearly half the passengers were ill—dramatically ill. Several were moaning and groaning, some were doubled up in pain, and two were unconscious. Fortunately there was a doctor on board, and he was helping the flight attendants. He came to the galley and said, "I'd better speak to the pilot. This is a severe case of food poisoning. I think we'd better land as soon as possible." "What caused it?" asked one of the flight attendants. "Well," replied the doctor, "I had the beef for dinner, and I'm fine. The passengers who chose the fish are sick." The flight attendant led him to the cockpit. She tried to open the door. "I think it's jammed," she said. The doctor helped her to push it open. The captain was lying behind the door. He was unconscious. The copilot was slumped across the controls, and the engineer was trying to revive him.

The doctor quickly examined the two men. "They just collapsed," said the engineer. "I don't feel too good myself." "Can you land the plane?" said the doctor. "Me? No, I'm not a pilot. We've got to revive them!" he replied. "The plane's on automatic pilot. We're O.K. for a couple of hours." "I don't know," said the doctor. "They could be out for a long time." "I'd better contact ground control," said the engineer. The doctor turned to the flight attendant. "Maybe you should make an announcement and try to find out if there's a pilot on board." "We can't do that!" she said. "It'll cause a general panic." "Then how are we going to get this thing down?" said the doctor.

Suddenly the flight attendant remembered something. "One of the passengers ... I overheard him saying that he'd been a pilot in the war. I'll get him." She found the man and asked him to come to the galley. "Didn't you say you used to be a pilot?" she asked. "Yes ... why? The pilot's all right, isn't he?" She led him to the cockpit. They explained the situation to him. "You mean, you want me to fly the plane?" he said. "You must be joking. I was a pilot, but I flew single-engined fighter planes, and that was fifteen years ago. This thing's got four engines!"

"Isn't there anybody else?" he asked. "I'm afraid not," said the flight attendant. The man sat down at the controls. His hands were shaking slightly. The engineer connected him to Air Traffic Control. They told him to keep flying on automatic pilot toward Anchorage and to wait for further instructions from an experienced pilot. An hour later the lights of Anchorage appeared on the horizon. He could see the lights of the runway shining brightly by a lake. Air Traffic Control told him to keep circling until the fuel gauge registered almost empty. This gave him a chance to get used to handling the controls. In the cabin the flight attendants and the doctor were busy attending to the sick. Several people were unconscious. The plane circled for over half an hour. The passengers had begun to realize that something was wrong. "What's going on? Why don't we land?" shouted a middle-aged man. "My wife's sick. We've got to get her to the hospital!" A woman began sobbing quietly. At last the plane started its descent. Suddenly there was a bump which shook the plane. "We're all going to die!" screamed a man. Even the flight attendants looked worried as panic began to spread through the plane. "It's all right!" someone said. "The pilot just lowered the landing gear, that's all." As the plane approached the runway they could see fire trucks and ambulances speeding alongside the runway with their lights flashing. There was a tremendous thump as the wheels hit the tarmac, bounced twice, raced along the runway, and screeched to a halt. The first airport truck was there in seconds. "That was nearly a perfect landing. Well done!" shouted the control tower. "Thanks," said the man. "Any chance of a job?"

THE CURIO SHOP

Anita Alvarado and Steve Weaver are antique dealers. They have a very successful business. They travel around the country buying antique furniture and paintings from flea markets, junk stores, and elderly people. Then they sell them at their store in Greenwich Village, a fashionable part of New York City. Today they're in a small town in South Carolina. Steve has just come out of a little curio shop, and he seems very excited.

Steve: Anita, we're in luck! There's a painting in there, a landscape. It's a good one. I thought it might be valuable, so I took a good look at the signature. It isn't very clear. I think it may be a Winslow Homer.

Anita: A Winslow Homer?! It can't be! They're all in museums. They're worth a fortune!

Steve: Well, someone found one a couple of years ago. This might be another one. It's dirty, and it isn't in very good condition.

Anita: How much do you think it's worth?

Steve: I don't know. It may be worth a million; it might even be worth more!

Anita: Be careful, Steve. We'd better use the old trick.

Steve: Yeah, right. There's a chair in the window. It must be worth about twenty dollars. I'll offer the old lady a hundred bucks for it. She'll be so happy that she won't think about the painting.

Anita: Don't say you want the painting; say you want the frame. O.K.?

Steve: Fine, you'd better wait in the van. I'd rather do this on my own.

Anita: Uh . . . Steve, check the signature before you give her a hundred bucks for the chair.

Steve: Don't worry, Anita. I know what I'm doing.

Mrs. Venable: I'll be with you in a minute.

Steve: I'm interested in that chair in the window.

Mrs. Venable: What? That old thing? It's been there for years!

Steve: It has? Uh . . . it's very nice. I think it could be Victorian.

Mrs. Venable: Really?

Steve: Yes, I think I'm right. I've seen one or two other chairs like it. I think I could get a good price for that in New York. I'll offer you a hundred dollars.

Mrs. Venable: A hundred dollars! You must be out of your mind!

Steve: No, no. It's a fair price.

Mrs. Venable: Well, then, it's yours.

Steve: There you are then, a hundred dollars. Good-bye. Oh, by the way, that painting's in a nice frame.

Mrs. Venable: It's a nice picture, honey. Late nineteenth century, I've heard.

Steve: Oh, no . . . no, it can't be. I've seen lots like it. It must be twentieth century. There's no market for them. Still, I could use the frame.

Mrs. Venable: All right. How much will you give me for it?

Steve: Uh . . . how about forty dollars?

Mrs. Venable: Oh, no, honey. It must be worth more than that. It came from the big house on the hill.

Steve: It did? Let me have another look at it. Yes, the frame really is nice. I'll give you two hundred.

Mrs. Venable: Oh my, I don't know what to do. You see, I like that painting myself.

Steve: All right, two hundred and fifty. That's my final offer.

Mrs. Venable: Let's say . . . two seventy-five?

Steve: O.K. It's a deal.

Mrs. Venable: Shall I wrap it up for you?

Steve: No, no. I have the van outside. It was nice doing business with you. Good-bye!

Mrs. Venable: Bye-bye, honey. Thank you. You come back to see us, you hear?

Mrs. Venable: Beauregard?

Mr. Venable: Yes, darling?

Mrs. Venable: I've sold another one of your imitation Winslow Homers. You'd better bring another one downstairs, if the paint's dry. The young gentleman who bought it seemed very happy with it.

Look at this:

I'm certain . . . I'm almost certain . . .	It must be . . .
I think it's possible . . .	It could be . . . It may be . . .
I think it's possible . . . (but a little less possible than "may")	It might be . . .
I think it's almost impossible . . . I think it's impossible . . .	It can't be . . . It couldn't be . . .

NOISY NEIGHBORS

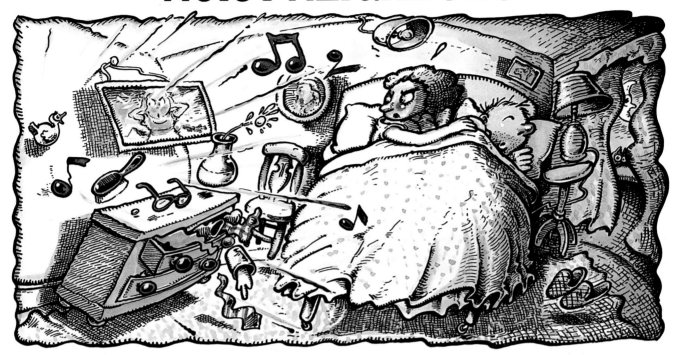

Harriet: Pssst! Ozzie! Ozzie! Wake up!

Ozzie: Huh? What? What's the matter? It can't be seven o'clock already!

Harriet: No. It's half past one. It's those people next door again. Listen!

Ozzie: Oh, yeah. They must be having another party.

Harriet: Listen to that! They must be waking up the whole block. And they have three young children. They couldn't be sleeping through that racket. It's disgusting! Somebody should call the police! Ozzie, wake up!

Ozzie: Huh? I wasn't asleep, dear. They're all laughing. They must be having a good time. They never invite us, do they?

Harriet: Ozzie!

Ozzie: Yes, dear. What is it now?

Harriet: Listen! They must be leaving.

Ozzie: Thank goodness for that! Maybe we'll get some sleep.

Harriet: I hope so. It's nearly three o'clock. Goodnight, dear. Oh, no! Now they're having a fight.

Ozzie: I'm not surprised. They always have fights after parties.

Harriet: Uh, oh! They must be throwing the dishes again.

Ozzie: No, I think that was a vase dear, or maybe the TV set—or both! They'll be sorry in the morning.

Harriet: Ozzie! Wake up!

Ozzie: Huh? Oh, what's that banging?

Harriet: He couldn't be hammering at this time of night.

Ozzie: What time is it?

Harriet: Four o'clock. What could they be doing at four o'clock in the morning?

Ozzie: I don't hear any voices. Go back to sleep, Harriet dear.

Harriet: Ozzie! Listen. There's someone in the backyard next door.

Ozzie: Huh? It must be the garbage man.

Harriet: No, it can't be. It's too early. It's only a quarter to five. Who could it be? I'd better take a look. Ooh! It's Howard Kennedy, and he's carrying a shovel.

Ozzie: Really? You don't think he's killed her, do you?

Harriet: Well, we haven't heard her voice for a while. No, she's probably sleeping.

Ozzie: But what could he be doing at this time of night?

Harriet: If he has killed her, he might be burying the body!

Ozzie: What?! You don't think so, do you?

Harriet: Well, he couldn't be planting tomatoes, could he? Do you think I should call the police?

Ozzie: No. Why don't you ask him what he's doing first!

Harriet: Hello there, Howard. You're up bright and early this morning.

Howard: I haven't been to bed yet. We had a party last night. I hope we didn't keep you awake.

Harriet: Oh, no, no. We didn't hear a thing, nothing at all. I slept like a log.

Howard: Well, it was a pretty noisy party. My wife knocked over the kids' tropical fish tank while we were cleaning up. The poor fish died. I'm just burying them before the kids wake up.

Exercise

What do you think your parents/brothers/sisters/friends are doing right now.

If you think you know what they are doing, answer with:

They must be doing this.
They couldn't be doing that.
They're probably doing this.

If you don't know, use:

They could/may/might be doing this.
or:
They're possibly doing this.

What about the President of the U.S./the Queen of England/the students in the class next door/the principal of the school/a famous movie or TV star/a famous sports celebrity.

A SPARKLING CAMP

It's a Friday afternoon in June at the Tukabatchee Summer Camp. The camp counselors are supposed to be working, but they aren't. The camp has to be ready for the first summer campers. They'll arrive tomorrow. The counselors have had lunch, and they're taking it easy in the counselors' lounge. The camp director has just opened the door. He's brought the duty roster with him, so he knows exactly what each of them should be doing.

Director: Hey, what's going on here?

Exercise 1
Look at Terri in the picture. Ask and answer about the other counselors.

1. *What's she doing?*
   She's lying on the sofa.
   She's smoking.
   She's watching TV.
2. *Should she be smoking?*
   No, she shouldn't.
   Should she be cutting the grass?
   Yes, she should.
3. *What should she be doing?*
   She should be cutting the grass.
   What shouldn't she be doing?

She shouldn't be lying on the sofa.
She shouldn't be smoking.
She shouldn't be watching TV.

Exercise 2
Terri ought to be cutting the grass.
She ought not to be smoking.
Write similar sentences about the other counselors.

Director: Terri! What are you doing?
Terri: I'm watching TV.
Director: And what are you supposed to be doing, Terri?
Terri: I'm not sure.
Director: Well, let me tell you, Terri. You're supposed to be cutting the grass.
Terri: Oh, right! I'm sorry. I forgot.
Director: When I come back, you'd better be cutting the grass. Do you hear me?
Terri: Yeah, yeah. I'm going.
Director: Get a move on, Terri. Remember the Tukabatchee motto: "A sparkling camp by the sparkling water."

Exercise 3
Make similar conversations between the director and the other counselors.

TUKABATCHEE SUMMER CAMP
"A Sparkling Camp by the Sparkling Water"
Counselors' Duties

Date: June 24

Counselor	Duty
Terri B.	cut grass
Kevin G.	paint canoes
Linda H.	clean swimming pool
Shawn M.	mark volleyball courts
Michelle S.	straighten up crafts room

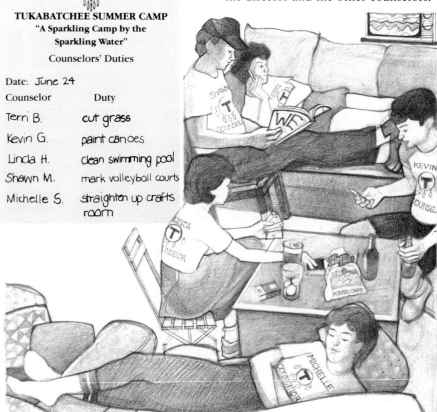

Look at this:

Exercise 4
Terri's cutting the grass.
She'd rather not be cutting the grass.
She'd rather be lying on the beach.
Make sentences about the other counselors.

Exercise 5
What are you doing?
What would you rather be doing?
Make five sentences.

One of the greatest mysteries of nature is the instinct to migrate. Every year millions of creatures feel the need to move for one reason or another. Most of us have seen the arrival or departure of migrating flocks of birds. Migration, however, is not confined to birds, but can be seen in reptiles (for example, turtles, frogs), insects (butterflies, locusts), fish (eels, salmon, tuna) and mammals (reindeer, seals, lemmings, whales, bats). Many of these creatures succeed in navigating over long distances. Just how they manage to do this still remains a mystery. There are several possibilities. They may navigate by using one or more of the following:

1. The sun.
2. The stars.
3. The earth's magnetic field. (When a small bar magnet is attached to a pigeon, it is unable to navigate.)
4. A sense of smell.
5. Geographical features. (Birds flying from South America to Canada seem to follow coastlines and valleys.)
6. Changes in temperature. (Salmon can detect a change in water temperature as small as .05 of a degree F.)
7. Sound. (Whales and bats seem to use sonar.)

Experiments suggest that these navigational abilities are partly instinctive. In one famous experiment a young seabird from the British Isles was taken across the Atlantic by plane to Boston, 3,200 miles away. It was released and was back in its nest twelve and a half days later.

The Arctic Tern

This seabird holds the record for long-distance migration. Arctic Tern breed in northern Canada, Greenland, northern Europe, Siberia, and Alaska. In late August they set off on an 11,000-mile journey which takes them south past the western coasts of Europe and Africa to the southern tip of Africa (9,000 miles in 90 days). They then fly around to the Indian

MIGRATION

Ocean and down to Antarctica, where they spend the Antarctic summer. On the way back they sometimes make a complete circle of Antarctica before returning to their breeding grounds. The round trip is about 22,000 miles in eight months (150 miles a day when they are flying.) The Arctic Tern sees more hours of daylight than any other creature because it experiences two summers a year—one in the Arctic region and one in the Antarctic. These regions have almost constant daylight in summer. One tern, which was tagged with a ring in Norway as a chick, died in exactly the same place, twenty-seven years later. Presumably, it had made the journey twenty-seven times.

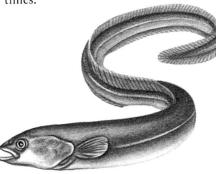

The European Freshwater Eel

European Freshwater Eels, which look like snakes but are really fish, begin and end their lives in the Sargasso Sea, southeast of Bermuda. As eggs and larvae they drift for three years towards

Europe, changing both shape and color as they reach the freshwater estuaries of European rivers. They spend the next nine to nineteen years in rivers, streams, lakes, and ponds. As they approach old age they seem to return to the Sargasso Sea to spawn. Many eels which have found their way into ponds and lakes come out of the water and travel over land, slithering through damp grass. When they reach the ocean, they make their way to the Sargasso, where they spawn and die. No eels make the journey twice. The eel has an acute sense of smell, which is used for navigation in local waters, but inherited memory seems the only explanation for their migration to the Sargasso.

The Lemming

The Brown Lemming is a small mammal (4–7 inches long) found all over the northern parts of North America and Europe. Lemmings usually make short, annual migrations in the spring, traveling by night and feeding and sleeping by day. Every three or four years, however, they make much longer migrations in large numbers. The lemming population seems to change over a three or four year cycle, from one lemming per acre to between 400 and 700 lemmings per acre. Migration seems to be a method of population control and is most spectacular in the well-known "mass suicides," where thousands of lemmings plunge over cliff tops into the sea and swim until they die of exhaustion. These "mass suicides" only occur infrequently and then only in Norway where mountains touch the sea. Nobody knows what makes them do it, but there are two theories. One is that migrating lemmings cross rivers and lakes and can't tell the difference between a river and the sea. The other more interesting theory is that they are migrating towards ancient breeding grounds which existed beneath the North Sea millions of years ago, when the sea level was lower.

MURDER IN NEW ORLEANS

Part 1

John Beresford Tifton was found dead on the floor of his study in the Tifton family mansion in New Orleans. He had been shot five times. The police have been called. There are six people in the house, and they all heard the shots at about four o'clock this afternoon. The police have taken statements and made the following notes about each of the six people.

Lydia Dubois Tifton, 62

Married to John Tifton for thirty-five years.
Handicapped—has been in a wheelchair since a riding accident twelve years ago.
Had a loud argument with Ruth Ellen Potts this morning.
Told Tifton to fire Ruth Ellen.
After long argument, Tifton refused to fire her.

Lydia Tifton's statement

I was in my room. I had the old den on the first floor turned into a bedroom for me because I can't walk. I was reading. I heard the shots; there were four or five. I wheeled myself into the hall. The study door was open. Ruth Ellen was standing in the doorway screaming. Benson was standing at the French windows. The gun was on the floor by Big Daddy.

Ruth Ellen Potts, 24

Tifton's private secretary.
Young, beautiful, intelligent—works to support her sick mother.
Has worked for Tifton for a year.
Report in a gossip column in today's *Picayune Times* says she had been seen with J. D. Tifton at a new disco, The Red Parrot, near the French Quarter.
Old Tifton was very upset about it. Threatened to fire her but didn't.

Ruth Ellen Potts's statement

I was in the living room writing some letters—actually job applications. I heard the shots and ran across the hall. The door to the study was open. There was poor, dear John—Mr. Tifton—lying in a pool of blood. I started screaming. Benson came in through the French windows; they were open. Then Lydia arrived. She didn't say a word. She just stared at me.

J.D. Tifton, 33

Tifton's only child.
Reputation as a gambler and member of the international jet set.
Thrown out of three colleges. Divorced by two wives.
Has large gambling debts.
Arrested last year for possession of drugs. Given suspended sentence.
Is heir to the Tifton fortune. Will inherit $25,000,000.
Old man Tifton had refused to let him have any more money.

J. D.'s statement

I was in the new den. I was playing a video game. Suddenly there were five shots. I thought it was Uncle Ike at target practice. Then I heard a scream. It sounded like Ruth Ellen; so I opened the connecting door to the study and saw Big Daddy lying there, Benson at the French windows, and Big Mama and Ruth Ellen together in the doorway to the hall. I couldn't believe my eyes.

Charles ("Cajun") Long, 29

Chauffer. Son of old man Tifton's ex-secretary. Often goes fishing with Dubois.
Wanted to marry Ruth Ellen Potts. Proposed to her, but she turned him down.
Has been in trouble with the police several times for fighting in bars.
Has violent temper.
Had argument with Tifton about a raise in pay earlier in the day.

Cajun Long's statement

I was working on the car. I heard shots, but old man Tifton and Ike—Mr. Dubois—have a little target practice sometimes. The police never bother them. Then I heard lots of screaming, so I went into the house through the back door to see what was happening. They were all there. I wasn't sorry. He deserved it. Everybody hated him.

Dwight ("Ike") Dubois, 60

Lydia Tifton's brother.
Was Olympic rifle shooting champion.
Drinks heavily.
Drives a Cadillac.
Doesn't work—spends time hunting and fishing.
Was manager of Pontchartrain Land Development Corporation, one of Tifton's companies.
Went to prison for two years when the company collapsed with debts of over $2 million after a big land scandal.
Has lived in the Tifton mansion since getting out of prison.

Dwight Dubois's statement

I was out by the pond, fishing in my usual spot. When I heard the shots, I hurried through the trees toward the house. I saw Benson running across the lawn toward the study. When I got there, everybody was in the room, except Cajun, the chauffer. Poor old Johnny was dead. I know a dead man when I see one. After all, I was in the army during the war.

Harold Benson, 65

Butler. Has worked for the Tifton family for nearly forty years.
Retires in two months.
Likes good wine and good food.
Takes Lydia Tifton out every day in her wheelchair.
Knows everything about the family.
Had long argument with old man Tifton in the morning.
Knows Ruth Ellen's mother very well.
Introduced Ruth Ellen to old man Tifton.

Benson's statement

I was about to take my afternoon walk. The doctor told me to walk twice a day for my heart. Anyway, I had just come out of the back door, and I was walking around the corner of the house when I heard shooting. I ran across the lawn to the French windows. I saw Mr. John's body and Miss Ruth Ellen in the doorway.

Part 2

Chief of Detectives Tony Damato is in charge of the case. Detective Sergeant Novak is his assistant. They're in the Tifton study.

Damato: Where is everybody?

Novak: They're all in the living room. Reyes is with them. What do you think?

Damato: It could have been any of them, couldn't it? We don't know what skeletons are in the closet! It might even have been all of them. Nobody seems very sad.

Novak: Yeah. Tifton wasn't exactly popular around here. Nobody liked him. It could have been an outsider.

Damato: No, Novak. It must have been one of them. Let's look at the evidence.

Novak: It seems to me that everybody has a motive, and nobody has an alibi. They all say they were alone when it happened.

Damato: Yes, and there are no fingerprints on the gun.

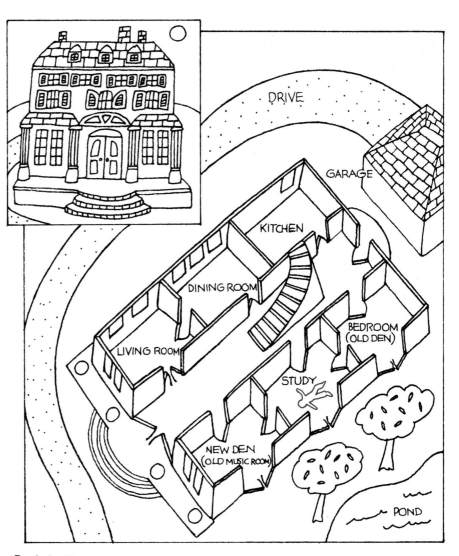

Lydia Tifton?

Novak: It couldn't have been her.

Damato: Why not?

Novak: Well, she's in a wheelchair. She can't move very fast. Anyway, they've been married for thirty-five years. It just couldn't have been her.

Damato: Most murders are committed by someone in the family, Novak, and that door goes into her room.

Novak: Right, but it was locked.

Damato: Doors have keys.

Novak: But why would she want to kill him?

Damato: Ruth Ellen Potts is a very attractive young woman. We don't know what was going on. The old woman might have been jealous.

Novak: But he was over sixty! He was old enough to be her father.

Damato: Hmm ... yes, but he was a good-looking man—and very rich and powerful.

Dwight Dubois?

Damato: What about Dubois, Novak? He's a weird guy.

Novak: I've been thinking about that. It couldn't have been him.

Damato: Why not?

Novak: Why would he need to shoot five times? He was a champion marksman. He could have killed him with one shot.

Damato: Maybe he did, Novak, maybe he did.

Novak: I don't follow.

Damato: There are a lot of things you don't follow, Novak. Maybe he's smarter than he looks.

Novak: But there's no motive.

Damato: There might have been. I mean there was the scandal with that land development company.

Novak: But he was down by the pond.

Damato: He might have been. He's a champion marksman. He could have shot him from the trees and thrown the gun into the room.

Novak: Oh, yeah. Do you really think so?

Damato: I don't know. It's just a theory.

Look at this:

Could	it have been	him?
		her?
		them?

It	must	have been	him.
	could(n't)		her.
	may (not)		them.
	might (not)		

Could	he	have	shot him?
	she		killed him?
	they		been the one(s)?

He	must	have	shot him.
She	could(n't)		killed him.
They	may (not)		been the one.
	might (not)		

Exercise

Discuss each character. Make a list of sentences about all six suspects. Who do you think did it? How? Why?

CONSUMER PROTECTION

Complaining about a defective product or about bad service is never easy. Most people don't like making scenes. However, when you buy consumer products, it is important to know your rights. In the United States, certain rights may be a little different from one state to another, but you have basic rights under federal law in any part of the country. The following information is taken from a pamphlet produced by the Federal Trade Commission. It gives advice to consumers.

Warranties: There Ought To Be a Law...

The Magnusson-Moss Warranty Act helps you *before* you buy by letting you see the warranties. Warranties on consumer products costing more than $15 must be available for you to look at before you buy so you can make comparisons and get the best warranty. And, the Warranty Act helps you *after* you buy by making it easier for you to force companies to keep their warranty promises.

Some Basic Points

Under the Warranty Act, all warranties must be easy to read and understand. All the conditions must be spelled out in writing. Be careful with spoken explanations. What the sales clerk says about the warranty is one thing; what's written may be another.

Note: The law doesn't require warranties except on certain products. If you buy a product "as is," you will have to pay for any repairs.

What Kinds of Warranties Are There?

Written Warranties.

There are two kinds of written warranties: Full and Limited.

A Full Warranty means all this:

- A defective product will be fixed or replaced free.
- It will be fixed within a reasonable time.
- You will not have to do anything unreasonable to get warranty service (such as ship a piano to the factory).
- The warranty is good for the whole warranty period, even for a second or third owner.
- If the product can't be fixed or hasn't been fixed after a reasonable number of tries, you get your choice of a new one or your money back.

But there is one important thing the word "Full" doesn't promise. A Full Warranty doesn't have to cover the whole product. It might cover only part of the product, like the picture tube of a TV. Or it might leave out some parts, like the tires on a car. Always check what parts the warranty covers.

A Limited Warranty gives you less than what a Full Warranty gives. "Limited" means "be careful — something's missing." For example a Limited Warranty might:

- Cover only parts, not labor.
- Allow a partial refund or credit according to the time that has passed since you bought the product.
- Require you to return a heavy product to the store for service.
- Cover only the original owner.
- Charge for handling.

A product can carry more than one written warranty. For example, it can have a Full Warranty on part of the product and a Limited Warranty on the rest.

Implied Warranties

These are rights under state law, not given by the company. All states have them. The most common implied warranty is the "warranty of merchantability." This means that the seller promises that the product you buy is fit for the ordinary uses of the product. For example, a reclining chair must recline; a toaster must toast. If it doesn't, you have a legal right to get your money back. Another implied warranty is the "warranty of fitness for a particular purpose." If a seller tells you that a product can be used for a special purpose, this advice is a warranty. For example, a seller who suggests a certain sleeping bag for zero-degree weather is promising that the sleeping bag will be suitable for zero degrees.

Implied warranties come automatically with every sale. If you get a written warranty, you get the implied warranties too.

Other warranties. Spoken promises and advertising can be warranties too. You have a legal right to get what the company promises.

If The Problem Isn't Solved

Your warranty rights don't run out at the end of the warranty period for problems you complained about during the warranty period. The company must still take care of those problems, no matter how long it takes.

How You Can Use Warranties

Read warranties before you buy to get the best deal. Sometimes it's better to pay more for a product with a better warranty. The extra money is like insurance, but remember that a warranty is only as good as the company that stands behind it. A 20-year warranty by a fly-by-night company might not be a help when you need it.

Read the warranty when a problem comes up. The warranty is a contract that spells out your rights. The company must do what it promises. Keep your receipt with your warranty. You might need it to prove the date you bought the product or that you were the original owner.

The Federal Trade Commission enforces the Warranty Act. To report violations of the law, write to the FTC, Warranties, Washington, DC 20580, or contact FTC Regional Offices in Atlanta, Boston, Chicago, Cleveland, Dallas, Denver, Los Angeles, San Francisco, and Seattle.

MAKING A COMPLAINT

174 Logan Drive
San Diego, CA 92013
May 22, 1984

Customer Service Dept.
Peers Lowbuck Co.
Chicago, IL 60606

Dear Sir or Madam:

Last week I bought a pocket calculator at your store in Anaheim, California. It seemed to work in the store. When I got home, I found it was defective. It performs arithmetic functions perfectly well, but the memory function does not operate. I took it back to your store in San Diego, but they refused to exchange it. They said that I would have to return it to the store where I bought it. This is impossible because I do not live in Anaheim. Enclosed please find the calculator along with the receipt, showing the price and date of purchase, and your guarantee.

Thank you for your attention to this matter.

Sincerely,

Gail Yamamura

(Mrs.) Gail Yamamura

Customer: Good morning. I'd like to speak to the manager.

Manager: I am the manager, sir. How can I help you?

Customer: Oh, yes. It's this radio. It doesn't work.

Manager: Hmm ... did you buy it here?

Customer: Pardon me? Of course I bought it here. Look, you turn it on and nothing happens.

Manager: May I see your receipt?

Customer: Receipt? I don't have one.

Manager: You must have gotten a receipt when you bought it.

Customer: I probably did. I must have thrown it away.

Manager: Uh huh. Well, do you have any other proof of purchase—the guarantee, for example?

Customer: No. It must have been in the box. I threw that away too.

Manager: Oh dear. You really ought to have kept it. We need to know the exact date of purchase.

Customer: What? I only bought it yesterday! That young man over there waited on me. Oh, I paid by credit card. I have my copy here.

Manager: Oh. All right then. Did you test the radio before you left the store?

Customer: Test it? No, it was in the original box. I expected it to work. It wasn't some cheap radio; it's a good brand.

Manager: You should have tested it.

Customer: Come on! Stop telling me what I should have done, and do something! Either give me my money back or give me another radio.

Manager: There's no need to get impatient, sir. Let me look at it. Hmm ... you see this little switch in the back?

Customer: Yes.

Manager: It's on "AC" and it should be on "DC." You really should have read the instructions.

Customer: Oh!

Exercise

> ### OWNER'S WARRANTY
> Digital Alarm Clock
> Model K9-12-B
> This clock has been inspected and tested in our factory and was shipped in perfect working order. If it fails to perform perfectly under normal conditions, return it to us in the original package, enclosing a copy of your receipt. We will repair it or replace it with a new one, free of charge.
> QUARTZ KLOX, P.O. Box 307, Fair Oaks, CA 95628

Write a letter of complaint. You bought the clock at a Goodworth store on Main Street in your town last week. It said "blue" on the box, but it was pink. The alarm doesn't seem to work. You paid cash, and you didn't keep the receipt.

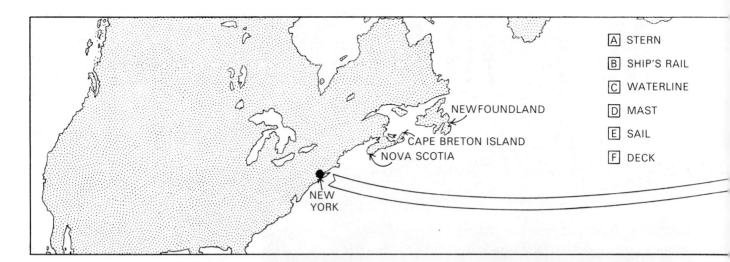

STERN
SHIP'S RAIL
WATERLINE
MAST
SAIL
DECK

NEWFOUNDLAND
CAPE BRETON ISLAND
NOVA SCOTIA
NEW YORK

THE "MARY CELESTE"

The *Mary Celeste* was built in 1861 in Nova Scotia, Canada, as a cargo-carrying sailing ship. When it was launched, it was given the name *Amazon*. It was not a lucky ship. The first captain died a few days after it was registered, and on its first voyage in 1862 it was badly damaged in a collision. While it was being repaired in port, it caught fire. In 1863 it crossed the Atlantic for the first time, and in the English Channel it collided with another ship which sank. The *Amazon* was badly damaged itself. Four years later, in 1867, it ran aground on Cape Breton Island, off the Canadian coast. The ship was almost completely wrecked and had to be rebuilt. It was then sold and the name was changed to the *Mary Celeste*. Sailors are very superstitious and dislike sailing on ships which have been unlucky or which have changed their names. Many sailors refused to sail on the *Mary Celeste*.

On November 5, 1872, the *Mary Celeste* left New York, carrying a cargo of industrial alcohol to Genoa in Italy. There were eleven people on board: Captain Briggs, his wife and two-year-old daughter, and a crew of eight. Briggs was an experienced captain and a very religious man. In his cabin there was a harmonium, which was used for playing hymns.

A month later the *Mary Celeste* was seen by another ship, the *Dei Gratia*, about halfway between the Azores and the Portuguese coast. Captain Moorhouse of the *Dei Gratia,* a friend of Captain Briggs, noticed that the ship was sailing strangely. When the *Mary Celeste* did not answer his signal, he decided to investigate. He sent a small boat to find out what was wrong.

The *Mary Celeste* was completely deserted.
• The only lifeboat was missing.
• All the sails were up and in good condition.
• All the cargo was there.
• The ship had obviously been through storms. The glass cover on the compass was broken.
• The windows of the deck cabins had been covered with wooden planks.
• There was 3 feet of water in the cargo hold, which was not enough to be dangerous.
• The water pumps were working perfectly.
• There was enough food for six months and plenty of fresh water.
• All the crew's personal possessions (clothes, boots, pipes and tobacco, etc.) were on board.
• There were toys on the captain's bed.
• There was food and drink on the cabin table.
• Only the navigation instruments and ship's papers were missing.
• The last entry in the ship's log book had been made eleven days earlier, about 600 miles west, but the ship had continued in a straight line.
• The forehatch was found open.

• There were two deep marks on the bow, near the waterline.
• There was a deep cut on the ship's rail, made by an axe.
• There were old brown bloodstains on the deck and on the captain's sword, which was in the cabin.

Captain Moorhouse put some sailors on the *Mary Celeste* who sailed it to Portugal. There was a long official investigation, but the story of what had happened on the ship, and what had happened to the crew, still remains a mystery. Captain Moorhouse and his crew were given the salvage money for bringing the ship to port. Many explanations have been suggested, but none of them have ever been proved.

Exercise
Find words which mean:
1. All the people working on a ship
2. The official, daily, written record of a ship's voyage
3. A religious song
4. Put a boat into the water
5. An instrument that shows the position of "north"
6. A musical instrument, like a small organ
7. A long, thin, narrow, flat piece of wood
8. Payment given to those who save other's property at sea
9. Goods carried on a ship
10. A machine for forcing water into or out of something

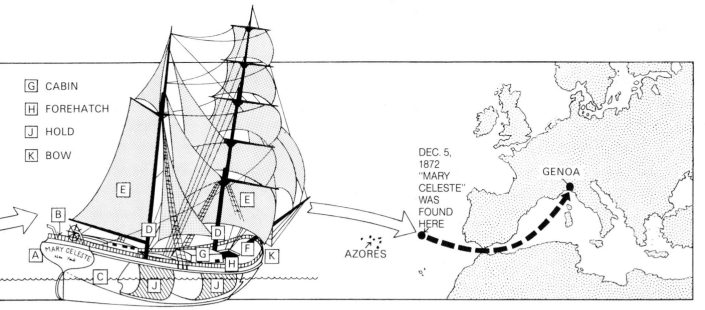

G CABIN
H FOREHATCH
J HOLD
K BOW

DEC. 5, 1872 "MARY CELESTE" WAS FOUND HERE

AZORES

GENOA

What do you think happened?

Sarah: I don't know what happened, but it must have happened suddenly.

Mark: Why do you think that?

Sarah: Think about it. There were toys on the captain's bed, weren't there? The child must have been playing, and they must have interrupted her suddenly.

Mark: Yes, that's true. And the food was on the table. They must have been eating or getting ready to eat.

Sarah: I'll tell you my theory. The lifeboat was missing, right? They could have been practicing their emergency drill. They must have gotten into the boat and launched it.

Mark: All right, but what happened to the boat?

Sarah: Well, they may have been rowing the lifeboat around the ship, and there must have been a gust of wind; then the ship could have moved forward and run down the lifeboat. That explains the marks on the bow.

Mark: Come on. They couldn't have all been sitting in the lifeboat. What about the captain? He should have been steering the ship!

Sarah: Well, he might have been watching the drill and jumped in to save the others.

Some possible explanations of why the crew abandoned the ship.

Amazingly, all of these have been suggested at some time:

1. There was water in the hold. The crew panicked and abandoned the ship because they thought it was going to sink. (Why? The captain was very experienced, and the ship was in good condition. The water pumps were working.)

2. The child fell into the sea. The mother jumped in to save her. They launched a lifeboat to rescue her. (All of them? Why?)

3. One of the barrels of alcohol was damaged. Perhaps there was a small explosion. The hatch cover was off, either because of the explosion or to let the gas escape. They thought all of the cargo might explode. (But there is not much evidence of an explosion.)

4. The last log entry was 600 miles west, near Santa Maria Island. Maybe the ship was in danger of running aground on the island. The crew left the ship in a storm. (How did the ship continue in a straight line for eleven days?)

5. There was no wind, so they got into the lifeboat to tow the ship. The rope broke. (Why were the woman and the child in the lifeboat? Surely the ship was too heavy.)

6. They saw an island which was not on the map and went to investigate. (All of them?)

7. A member of the crew had a terrible, infectious disease. The others left to escape from it. The one with the disease killed himself.

What about the lifeboat?

If the crew left the ship by lifeboat, what happened to them?

1. It could have sunk in a storm.

2. The ship itself could have run down the lifeboat.

3. It could have drifted away, and all of them could have died of hunger and thirst.

4. They might have reached land. They were robbed and killed there.

5. A whale or sharks might even have overturned the boat.

One, or all of them, went crazy.

1. They drank some of the industrial alcohol. There was a fight. Some were killed; the others left. (But industrial alcohol is very poisonous.)

2. The cook was crazy and poisoned everybody. Then he killed himself after throwing the bodies into the sea.

3. The captain had an attack of religious mania, killed everybody, then himself.

4. There was a fungus called "ergot" in the bread. This is a fungus which can grow on rye bread. It is very similar to the drug LSD. Whole villages had been poisoned in this way in medieval Europe.

Crime.

1. The *Dei Gratia* attacked the *Mary Celeste* and killed everybody.

2. Pirates attacked and killed them.

3. There was a mutiny (a revolt against the captain of a ship). Two of the members of the crew were criminals. There was a fight. Some were killed. The others left.

4. Mrs. Briggs fell in love with a crew member. Again there was a fight.

5. The crew of the *Mary Celeste* attacked and robbed another ship and left on the other ship with its cargo. (Which other ship? There are no records.)

6. They found an abandoned ship with a valuable cargo and stole it.

7. Captain Briggs and Captain Moorhouse planned everything together for the salvage money. The ship was never abandoned. None of the story was true.

Outside forces.

1. A spaceship from another planet took everybody away.

2. A giant wave or a tornado knocked them all from the deck.

3. A sea monster (a giant octopus or sea serpent) attacked the ship.

4. Men living below the sea attacked the ship when it passed over the old site of Atlantis.

SPECULATION

1 △

Look at this:

He	must	be	crazy.
She	could	have been	at home.
They	may		
It	might	be doing	something.
	can't	have done	
	couldn't	have been doing	

Make as many sentences as possible about each of the pictures.

2 △

3 △

4 △

Unit 30

5△

6△

7△

8△

9△

11△

10
△

12△

Unit 30

APOLOGIES

C: Excuse me. Would you mind putting out your cigarette?
D: I beg your pardon?
C: This is the no-smoking section.
D: It is? I asked for the smoking section.
C: The smoking section is back there.
D: Oh, you're right. I'm awfully sorry.

G: Hey, you!
H: Are you talking to me?
G: Yes, you. What do you think you're doing?
H: Huh? I'm just waiting for the bus.
G: Can't you see there's a line?
H: Oh, there is? I'm sorry. I didn't mean to butt in. I didn't realize there was a line.

A: Hello?
B: Hi, Rafael. This is Alex.
A: Oh. Hi. Did you get home all right?
B: Yeah, thanks, but I wanted to apologize for last night.
A: Don't worry about it.
B: But your carpet! It must be ruined. It was so dumb of me to put my coffee on the floor.
A: Come on, Alex, forget it.
B: But it must have made a really ugly stain.
A: Look, it's nothing. I was upset at first, but it doesn't look so bad this morning.
B: Anyway, I want to pay for the cleaning.
A: Listen, Alex, it's no big deal. Accidents happen—at parties especially. I don't want to hear another word about it, O.K.?
B: Well, if you say so, but I really am sorry.
A: See you on Monday. Bye now.

E: Oh! Good morning, Mary Ann.
F: Good afternoon, Sharon. Late again, I see.
E: (Sigh) Yes. I'm sorry. I couldn't find a parking place.
F: Maybe you should have left home earlier.
E: Yes, I know. It won't happen again, Mary Ann.
F: It'd better not, Sharon. This is the third time this week.

I: Are you all right?
J: Yes, I'm O.K., but what about my car?
I: There doesn't seem to be too much damage.
J: Let me see . . . look at that! This is a brand new car! You shouldn't have been going so fast.
I: Well, it wasn't my fault.
J: It wasn't your fault?! What do you mean, it wasn't your fault? I had the right of way.
I: As a matter of fact you didn't. You shouldn't have come out like that.
J: Why not? There's no sign.
I: Then what's that?
J: Oh. A stop sign. I must have missed it.
I: Well, you should have been more careful. You could have gotten us all killed.
J: Yes, I see that now. I'm sorry. What else can I say?
I: Just thank God nobody's hurt. Here come the police. You'd better explain it to them.

THEY DIDN'T STOP TO TELL ME!

Police examine abandoned trucks in Bedford.

TRUCK HIJACKED IN BEDFORD
$100,000 Cargo Stolen

A truck carrying television sets, video recorders, microwave ovens, radios, business machines, and vacuum cleaners valued at over $100,000 was hijacked yesterday morning. The truck belonged to the Ruby Star Company, and the driver, Nicolas Estrella, was making deliveries to customers in the Bedford section.

This is the thirty-seventh truck hijacking in the first five months of this year. Over the last four years there have been 386 hijackings in the metropolitan area. The cargoes have ranged from 200,000 labels for Sergio Potentes jeans to Louise Nettlesome sculptures, from meat and cheese to champagne.

Drivers have been warned to be careful about locking their doors and have been warned not to pick up hitchhikers. Some insurance investigators believe that as many as one-third of these cases are not hijackings at all. They believe that dishonest drivers steal their own cargoes. The police point to the other culprits in these cases of urban thievery.

"The retail store owners who buy stolen goods make very big profits. They are the real criminals," said Police Capt. Mel Torino. "The hijackers steal because they can sell."

The hijackers seem to be both well-organized and well-informed. They concentrate on trucks carrying cargoes that can be sold quickly for cash. (continued on page A6)

Police Captain Mel Torino is questioning Nicolas Estrella, the driver of the hijacked Ruby Star truck.

Captain: Have a seat, Mr. Estrella. Cigarette?

Mr. Estrella: No, thanks, Captain. I'm trying to stop smoking.

Captain: Let's start at the beginning again. How did you lose your truck?

Mr. Estrella: You know the story already.

Captain: I'm sorry to do this, but I'm kind of slow. Tell me again.

Mr. Estrella: O.K. I was making deliveries in Bedford. The truck was loaded with TVs and radios.

Captain: Uh huh. So you drove to the Bedford section from the Ruby Star warehouse.

Mr. Estrella: Right. About 10 o'clock I made a delivery on Boyle Street. I'd finished and I was driving up Boyle when I saw a coffee shop.

Captain: So you decided to stop.

Mr. Estrella: That's right. I stopped to get a cup of coffee to go.

Captain: Go on.

Mr. Estrella: It didn't take me more than three minutes. I started walking back to the truck and . . .

Captain: Did you see anybody near the truck?

Mr. Estrella: No, nobody. So anyway, I decided to make a phone call.

Captain: A phone call?

Mr. Estrella: You can check that. I passed a magazine stand and I stopped to get change.

Captain: O.K. Then what?

Mr. Estrella: Well, I was talking to my wife when I saw the truck going down the street. I couldn't believe my eyes. I dropped the phone and ran down the street. But they were moving fast. I couldn't catch up.

Captain: Did you remember to lock the cab door?

Mr. Estrella: Yes, I always remember to lock it! I'm not that stupid!

Captain: O.K., O.K., take it easy. Can you actually remember locking it this time?

Mr. Estrella: Yes, definitely.

Captain: How can you be so sure?

Mr. Estrella: Well, I remember putting the key in the lock. It was all wet and dirty. It was raining, and I had dropped it in a puddle.

Captain: What about the door on the other side. Did you remember to check it?

Mr. Estrella: I don't actually remember checking it. But it's always locked, and I never use it.

Captain: But you don't remember checking it?

Mr. Estrella: No, not really. Maybe I forgot to check it.

Captain: So it could have been open.

Mr. Estrella: Yes, I guess so. But I'd bet anything it wasn't.

Captain: So what's your theory?

Mr. Estrella: They must have had keys. They started the engine, didn't they?

Captain: How did they get the keys?

Mr. Estrella: Don't ask me. I have no idea. They didn't stop to tell me!

Look at this:

He was driving. He stopped. He got some coffee.

A. *What did he stop doing? He stopped driving.*
B. *What did he stop to do? He stopped to get some coffee.*

Exercise 1
Ask two questions and give answers.
1. He was driving. He stopped. He bought some gas.
2. He was watching the truck. He stopped. He made a phone call.
3. He was talking to his wife. He stopped. He ran down the street.

Look at this:

I drove a car for the first time when I was sixteen. I was so nervous but so happy that day!
I remember driving a car for the first time.

I was going to mail this letter. I still have it.
I didn't remember to mail it.
I forgot to mail it.

Exercise 2
Make sentences.
1. I should have turned off the light. It's still on.
2. I read about the crime in the newspaper. I can remember it clearly.
3. There's a movie on TV tonight. I saw it at a theater ten years ago.
4. They ought to have done their homework. The teacher's very upset.

Unit 32

JOHN LENNON 1940-1980

John Lennon was murdered just before 11 p.m. on December 8, 1980, outside the Dakota, an apartment building where he lived in New York City. He had just gotten out of a car and was walking to the entrance when a voice called, "Mr. Lennon." Lennon turned and was shot five times. The killer threw his gun down and stood there smiling. "Do you know what you just did?" shouted the doorman. "I just shot John Lennon," the killer replied. Lennon was rushed to the hospital in a police car, but it was too late. The killer was 25 year-old Mark Chapman from Hawaii. Earlier the same evening he had asked Lennon for his autograph. In fact, he had been hanging around outside the apartment building for several days. Chapman was a fan of Lennon and had tried to imitate him in many ways. It is said that he even believed that he was John Lennon.

Biographical Notes

1940 Born in Liverpool, England.
1942 Lennon family deserted by father. Mother leaves. John brought up by aunt.
1956 Forms rock band at school.
1957 Student at Liverpool College of Art.
1958 Mother killed in car accident.
1960 Goes professional as one of "The Beatles" (Lennon, McCartney, Harrison, Best, Sutcliffe). Plays in Hamburg, Germany.
1961 Plays in Hamburg and Liverpool. Sutcliffe (Lennon's best friend) dies of brain tumor. Brian Epstein begins to manage the Beatles.
1962 Ringo Starr replaces Pete Best as Beatles drummer. Married Cynthia Powell, an art student. Beatles' first record "Love Me Do." First TV appearance.

1963 Three records Number 1 in British Top 20. Incredible popularity. Son Julian born.
1964 First hit record in U.S. "I Want to Hold Your Hand." Two U.S. tours. In April, Beatles' records Number 1, 2, 3, 4, and 5 in U.S. Top 20. First movie *A Hard Day's Night*. First book.
1965 *Help!* Beatles' second movie. Beatlemania at its height. U.S. tour. Huge audiences in sports stadiums. Beatles receive MBE (special honorary award) from Queen Elizabeth.

1966 Lennon in movie *How I Won the War*—not a musical. Meets Yoko Ono, Japanese avant-garde artist.
1967 "Sergeant Pepper"—Beatles' most famous album. All the Beatles interested in meditation. Manager Brian Epstein found dead from overdose of sleeping pills.
1968 In India with Beatles for meditation. Beatles' company, Apple, founded. Lennon art exhibit "You Are Here." Lennon divorced by wife.
1969 Beatles' movie *Let It Be*. Rumors of quarrels about money. Talk of Beatles breaking up. Beatles' last public performance on roof of Apple Building. Lennon and Yoko marry. He 29, she 36. Lennon still recording with Beatles but some work solo.
1970 McCartney leaves Beatles. Others start solo careers.
1971 Lennon's album "Imagine"—most successful album. Lennon and Yoko Ono in New York one-room studio apartment.
1972 Charity concerts.
1973 Lennon and Yoko Ono separate. Lennon in Los Angeles. Lennon ordered to leave U.S.—protests and appeals.
1974 Drinking problems—still fighting deportation.
1975 Lennon and Yoko Ono together again in New York. Permission to stay in U.S. Son Sean born October 9 (Lennon's birthday).
1976 Retires from public life. Extensive travel. Business affairs managed by Yoko Ono.
1976 Full-time father. Very close relationship with son. Owns seven apartments in same building—one for cold storage of fur coats.
1980 First record in six years. Album "Double Fantasy." Single "Starting Over." Good reviews from critics. Many said it was "a new beginning." Dec. 8 Lennon murdered. Massive media coverage. TV and radio programs interrupted to give news. Record companies on overtime to meet demand for records.
1981 Three records in Top 20 charts: "(Just Like) Starting Over," "Imagine," and "Woman."
1984 Lennon's last album, "Milk and Honey" released. "Nobody Told Me" reaches Top 20.

KIDNAPPED

Dr. Pamela Crane-Newton and Dr. Daniel Newton work at the same hospital in Phoenix, Arizona. Pamela is a cardiologist, and Daniel is a neurosurgeon. They usually come home together at six and have dinner with their daughter, Caroline. Tonight the house was dark when they arrived, and there was no sign of Caroline. On the floor, near the door, there was a note. Pamela picked it up, read it, and tears came to her eyes.

Daniel: Pamela, what's wrong? Is it from Caroline?

Pamela: No ... yes ... no. She ... (sob) ... She's been kidnapped!

Daniel: Kidnapped! Let me see that ... Oh, no! Oh, my God! (Sob) No, no, no!

Pamela: I'll call the police.

Daniel: No, Pamela! Don't touch the phone!

Pamela: Oh yes, the note says not to. Let's read it again—carefully.

Daniel: A million dollars!

Pamela: How long will it take us to get that much cash together?

Daniel: I don't know. Maybe we should call the police.

Pamela: No, Daniel. If the kidnappers find out, they'll kill her.

Daniel: But we'll have to borrow the money. If we don't tell the police, the bank won't let us have it.

Pamela: But remember what the note says. Unless we do exactly as they say, we may never see her again.

Daniel: Hello?

Voice: Did you find our note?

Daniel: Yes. We found it.

Voice: Have you told the police?

Daniel: No, we ... No, not yet.

Voice: You'd better not. When can you get the money?

Daniel: We need a few days.

Voice: You have one day.

Daniel: How do we know that Caroline is still alive?

Voice: You don't. You'll have to trust us. Get the money by tomorrow night. You'll hear from us again.

Daniel: If you harm a hair on her head, I'll ... I'll ...

WE have your daughter
She is safe and sound
We WANT $1,000,000
IF YOU give us the money
she will be OK Don't call
the police or we'll kill her
IF you try to contact them WE'LL know
If you don't follow our
instructions your Daughter will die
Unless you PAY up you'll never
see HER again

Exercise 1

1. If you were in Daniel and Pamela's place, would you call the police?
2. If you were in the kidnappers' place, how would you arrange to get the money?
3. If you were Daniel and Pamela, what would you do?
4. If you were the police, what would you do?

Exercise 2

A: *Give me the money!*
B: *Why should I?*
A: *If you don't give me the money, I'll kill you.*
B: *What?! You're crazy!*
A: *Maybe, but unless you give me the money, I'll kill you.*

Now look at the pictures, and make similar conversations.

STOP SMOKING OR YOU WON'T LIVE VERY LONG.

MARRY ME OR I'LL KILL MYSELF.

Exercise 3

Look at Exercise 2.
What would you do in the three situations?
If I were him, I'd give him the money.
If I were him, I'd hide under the counter.
If I were him, I'd pull the alarm.

HAVE YOU SEEN THIS AD?

Mike: Wendy, have you seen this ad?

Wendy: Yeah. It looks great, doesn't it? I called them an hour ago. They'll call back if they want me.

Mike: Oh, they'll want you for sure. I mean you have beautiful hair.

Wendy: I hope so. If I go, I'll get a new hairdo—and have a lot of fun too.

Louis: Pablo, look at this.

Pablo: Oh yeah, I've seen it. I'm going to call tomorrow.

Louis: It sounds very exciting, and you have a decent car.

Pablo: Uh huh. There are some disadvantages.

Louis: Every job has disadvantages, but you're always complaining about the job you have now.

Pablo: Oh, I don't know. I'm willing to try it. But I won't take it if they don't pay the phone bill!

Roger: Tina, what do you think of this ad?

Tina: Didn't I tell you? It was in last Sunday's paper too. I called. I have an interview tomorrow.

Roger: Do you think you'll get it?

Tina: They seemed very interested on the phone. I think they'll offer me the job.

Roger: So you're going to Mandanga!

Tina: I didn't say that. I won't take the job unless they give me a round trip ticket. It'll be hard work, and I won't go unless they offer me a good salary.

Sandy: Hey, Bill, look at this ad.

Bill: Hmm . . . It looks like fun. Why don't you call them up?

Sandy: I'd love to, but it's a waste of time. My hair's just too short.

Bill: Well, I like it the way it is. Anyway, you don't know what they might do. Hair standing up in spikes is really fashionable now.

Sandy: Oh, Bill, that wouldn't bother me. If I had longer hair, I'd call them up. Actually, *your* hair is pretty long now . . .

Kathy: Lynn, did you see this?

Lynn: Yeah. You aren't interested, are you?

Kathy: What! Me? I wasn't born yesterday! There are too many things wrong with it.

Lynn: Like what?

Kathy: I wouldn't take a job like that! You wouldn't have any security. You wouldn't earn anything if you didn't work all day long every day. And I wouldn't take a job in sales if they didn't provide the car.

Lynn: Yeah, and look at the address—some hotel. I'd never work for a company if they didn't even have an office.

Kitty: There's a job in Mandanga in the paper.

Terry: Yeah, I know. I wouldn't dream of taking it.

Kitty: Why not? You've been looking for a job in a foreign country.

Terry: It's slave labor, isn't it? One night off a week.

Kitty: But the money might be good.

Terry: Hmph! I wouldn't take it unless they paid me a really good salary with a longer vacation and more free time. And I certainly wouldn't go off to a place like Mandanga unless my ticket was round trip!

Exercise

Could you ever kill a person?
Not unless they tried to kill me.
I wouldn't kill anybody unless they tried to kill me.
What about these things?
Would you ever steal food/rob a bank/hit someone/eat a dog or cat/jump from a high building/take your clothes off in the street/go sky diving (with a parachute)/have a heart transplant?

Look at this:

I'm interested. I've applied.	I'm not interested. I haven't applied.
I'll accept the job if they offer enough money.	I'd apply if they offered more money.
I won't accept the job if they don't pay more.	I wouldn't accept the job if they didn't offer enough.
I won't accept the job unless they pay more.	I wouldn't accept the job unless they offered more.

Unit 35

"Good evening. This is Ted Cooper with MBS Late Night Report. Tonight, in our first segment, we're looking again at the problem of the world's limited energy resources. Nobody knows exactly how much fuel is left, but pessimistic forecasts say that there is only enough coal for 450 years and enough natural gas for 50 years and that oil might run out in 30 years. Obviously we have to do something, and we have to do it soon. Debate continues about the use of nuclear power to solve this crisis. First, we go by satellite to the studios of WLNN in Boston to hear from Professor William White of the New England Institute of Technology."

"Well, Mr. Cooper, we are in a long-range energy crisis. With lower oil prices people have forgotten that, as you said, fossil fuels—coal, oil and gas—are running out. The tragedy is that fossil fuels are far too valuable to waste on the production of electricity. Just think of all the things we make from oil! If we don't start conserving these things now, it will be too late. And nuclear power is the only real alternative. We are getting some electricity from nuclear power plants already. If we invest in further research now, we'll be ready to face the future. There's been a lot of protest lately against nuclear power—some people will protest anything—but nuclear power plants are not as dangerous as some people say. It's far more dangerous to work down in a coal mine or on an offshore oil rig. Safety regulations in nuclear power plants are very strict.

"If we spent money on research now, we could develop plants which create their own fuel and burn their own waste. In many parts of the world where there are no fossil fuels, nuclear power is the only alternative. If you accept that we need electricity, then we will need nuclear energy. Just imagine what the world would be like if we didn't have electricity—no heating, no lighting, no industry, no radio or TV. Just think about the ways you use electricity every day. Surely we don't want to go back to the Stone Age. That's what will happen if we turn our backs on nuclear research."

"Thank you, Professor White. Now we join our affiliate KJEM in San Francisco, where Jean Black is waiting to give us the position of CANE, the Campaign Against Nuclear Energy."

"Ted, I must disagree totally with

ENERGY CRISIS

Professor White. Let's look at the facts. First, there is no perfect machine. I mean, why do planes crash? Machines fail. People make mistakes. What would happen if there were a serious nuclear accident? And an accident is inevitable—sooner or later. Huge areas would be evacuated, and they could remain contaminated with radioactivity for years, and not a penny in compensation! No insurance company covers nuclear risks. There are accidents all the time. If the nuclear industry didn't keep them quiet, there would be a public outcry. Radioactivity causes cancer and may affect future generations.

"Next, nuclear waste. There is no technology for absolutely safe disposal. Some of this waste will remain radioactive for thousands of years. Is that what you want to leave to your children? And their children's children?

"Next, terrorism. Terrorists could blackmail the whole country if they captured a reactor. The Savannah River nuclear plant, and Professor White knows this very well, lost (yes, lost!) enough plutonium between 1955 and 1978 to make 18 (18!) atomic

bombs. Where is it? Who has it? I believe that nuclear energy is expensive, dangerous, evil, and most of all, absolutely unnecessary. I think your next guest will be saying more about that."

"Yes, thank you, Ms. Black, you're right. By satellite we now join Dr. Catalina Burgos at WFAM in Chicago. Dr. Burgos is the author of several books on alternative technology."

"Hello, Mr. Cooper. I'd like to begin by agreeing with Jean. We can develop alternative sources of power, and unless we try we'll never succeed. Instead of burning fossil fuels we should be concentrating on more economic uses of electricity, because electricity can be produced from any source of energy. If we didn't waste so much energy, our resources would last longer. You can save more energy by conservation than you can produce for the same money. Unless we do research on solar energy, wind power, wave power, tidal power, hydroelectric projects, etc., our fossil fuels will run out, and we'll all freeze or starve to death. Other countries are spending much more than we do on research, and don't forget that energy from the sun, the waves, and the wind lasts forever. We really won't survive unless we start working on cleaner, safer sources of energy."

"Thank you very much, Dr. Burgos. Our final speaker on the subject of energy is in the studios of WGMT in Washington, D.C. He is Joseph Huang, Under Secretary of Energy. Mr. Huang."

"I've been listening to the other speakers with great interest. By the way, I don't agree with some of the estimates of world energy reserves. More oil and gas is being discovered all the time. If we listened to the pessimists (and there are a lot of them around) none of us would sleep at night. In the short run, we must continue to rely on the fossil fuels—oil, coal, and gas. But we must also look to the future. Our policy must be flexible. Unless we thought new research was necessary, we wouldn't be spending money on it. After all, we wouldn't have a Department of Energy unless most people thought it was important. The big question is where to spend the money—on conservation of present resources or on research into new forms of power. But I'm fairly optimistic. I wouldn't be in this job unless I were an optimist!"

Unit 36

WHAT WOULD YOU HAVE DONE?

THE READER'S PAGE

What would you have done?

Last week we invited you, the readers, to write and tell us about things that had happened to you, or things that you had heard about. We wanted stories where people just didn't know what to do next! Here are the stories that interested us the most!

That's my beer...or was

I was in a bar in a small Western town. I had just been served a glass of beer. Suddenly this huge man — he looked like a boxer — came over, picked up my beer, drank it, banged the glass down on the table, stared at me, and then walked away without saying anything. I suppose I should have said something, but I was scared stiff! I didn't know what to do! What would you have done?
Stanley Wempe • Carbondale, IL

In deep water

I was driving through Oregon on my vacation. It was a very hot day, and I stopped at a small deserted beach. I didn't have my bathing suit with me, but it was early in the morning and there were no people or houses in sight. So I took off my clothes and swam out in the ocean in my underwear. I'm a very strong swimmer. I floated on my back, closed my eyes, and relaxed in the water. When I looked back at the beach, several cars had arrived and there were twenty or thirty people sitting on the sand having a picnic! What would you have done?
Jane Dare • Spokane, WA

That's a no-no

I heard a great story about the Rev. Billy Cracker. He'd gone to

London to speak at a large meeting. Anyway, when he stepped off the plane there were a lot of reporters and TV cameras. The first question one of the reporters asked was, "Do you intend to visit any nightclubs in London?" Rev. Cracker smiled at the reporter. "Are there any nightclubs in London?" he answered innocently. The next morning the headline in one of the London papers was "Cracker's first question on arrival in London — Are there any nightclubs?" How would you have felt?
Rev. Aural Richards • Columbia, SC

Strangers in the night

My story isn't funny at all. It was a very frightening experience. You

see, one night I woke up suddenly. I heard the tinkle of broken glass from downstairs, and I heard the window opening. Then I heard two voices! My wife woke up too. She told me to do something. A couple of days before there had been a report about a burglary in the local paper. The burglars had been interrupted, and they had beaten up the homeowner. They'd nearly killed him. I was trembling with fear. I just didn't know what to do. In the end, I didn't go down, and they stole the sterling silverware we had inherited from my mother. Was I right? What would you have done?
Lorenzo Machado • Abeline, TX

Deep fried

I had parked my car at a local shopping mall, and I was taking a

short cut through the side door of a restaurant. Halfway across the restaurant, I spotted my father eating a hamburger and french fries — he often eats there. I sneaked up behind him, put my hand over his shoulder, took a french fry off the plate, dipped it in catsup and ate it. Then I realized that the man was not my father! I was so embarrassed! I couldn't say a word! What would you have done?
Cheryl Redburn • Minneapolis, MN

Or else

I'd just parked my car on a street near the football stadium in Des Moines. It was ten minutes before the start of the game and I was in a hurry. Two little boys came up to me and said, "Give us $5 and we'll watch your car while you're at the game." I told them to clear out, and one of them looked at me with big, round, innocent eyes and said, "Unless you give us the money, something might happen to your car while you're away. You know, a scratch or a flat tire. Something like that." I was furious! What would you have done?
Helen Furie • Des Moines, IO

Honesty is the best policy

I couldn't believe a story I heard the other day. It seems that a woman had just bought a house in Burlingon, Vermont. She wanted to insulate the roof, so she and her son climbed up into the attic. There, under the hot water tank, was $50,000 in cash! They turned in the money to the police. Would you have reported the find? What would you have done?
Francine Marasco • Waterbury, VT

Look at this:

Would you have said anything?
What would you have done?

I	'd	have	said	something.
	would		done	
	wouldn't			anything.

Exercise 1
Make sentences like this about each of the seven stories.

Exercise 2
Tell the story of an interesting, surprising, or embarrassing experience you have had or heard about.

A BAD DAY AT THE OFFICE

Margot: What was wrong with you this morning?

Tim: Wrong with me? I'm sorry, Margot, I don't know what you mean.

Margot: You walked straight past me. You didn't say a word!

Tim: Really? Where?

Margot: It was just by that newsstand on 34th Street.

Tim: I'm really sorry, Margot. I just didn't see you.

Margot: Come on, Tim. You must have. I was waving!

Tim: No, honestly, I didn't see you. If I had seen you, I would've said hello.

Exercise 1
He didn't see her. He didn't say "hello."
If he had seen her, he would have said "hello."
Do the same:
1. He didn't recognize her. He didn't stop.
2. He didn't notice her. He didn't stop.
3. He didn't see her waving. He didn't wave back.

Peggy: Tim, have you sent that telex to Japan?

Tim: No, I haven't.

Peggy: Why haven't you done it yet? It's urgent.

Tim: Because you didn't ask me to do it.

Peggy: I didn't?

Tim: No, you didn't. If you had asked me, I'd have sent it.

Exercise 2
Have you sent the telex?
If you had asked me, I would have sent it.
Do the same:
1. Have you mailed the letters?
2. Have you photocopied the report?
3. Have you typed the contract?

Connie: Did you see a letter from Brazil on my desk?

Tim: Yes, here it is.

Connie: Oh, good. Where's the envelope?

Tim: I threw it away. Why?

Connie: It had some nice stamps on it. I wanted it for my uncle. He collects stamps.

Tim: Gee, Connie, if I'd known . . .

Connie: It's no big deal.

Tim: I would've kept it if I'd known.

Exercise 3
I didn't keep it.
I would have kept it if I had known.
Do the same:
1. I didn't call.
2. I didn't give it to you.
3. I didn't put it in the drawer.

Tim: What's the matter, Debbie. You don't look well.

Debbie: No. I've had a terrible cold. I've been in bed all weekend, but it's better today.

Tim: Hmm . . . I had a bad cold last week.

Debbie: I know, and you gave it to everyone in the office. I wouldn't have come to work if I'd had a cold like that.

Exercise 4
He had a bad cold, but he came to work.
I wouldn't have come to work if I had had a cold.
Do the same:
1. She had a headache, but she stayed at work.
2. He had a sore throat, but he worked all day.
3. She had a toothache, but she didn't go to the dentist.

Peggy: Tim?

Tim: Yes?

Peggy: Did you type this letter or did Akiko do it?

Tim: I did. Why? Is there something wrong with it?

Peggy: Take a look. This should be $400,000. You typed $40,000.

Tim: Oh yeah. I'm really sorry.

Peggy: And you misspelled the customer's name. It should be "Snelling," not "Smelling."

Tim: (Laugh) Oh, no! Did I put that?

Peggy: It's not funny, Tim. If I hadn't noticed it, we could have lost the order.

Exercise 5
She noticed the error. They didn't lose the order.
If she hadn't noticed the error, they could have lost the order.
Do the same:
1. She noticed the spelling mistake. They didn't upset the customer.
2. She saw it in time. They didn't send the letter.
3. She checked the letter. They didn't mail it.

Henry: Hi, Tim. Did you have a good day today?

Tim: No, not really. I'm glad it's over. Everything went wrong.

Henry: Really?

Tim: Yeah, I made a lot of mistakes in typing, then I forgot to send a telex, and Margot got upset because I ignored her on the street.

Henry: Why was that?

Tim: It was that party last night. If I hadn't gone to bed late, it wouldn't have been such an awful day. I'm going to make it an early night tonight.

Exercise 6
I went to a party./I went to bed late./I forgot to set the alarm./I got up late./I missed the bus./I was late for work./I've had a bad day./I forgot to send a telex./I made a mistake in typing.
If I hadn't gone to the party, none of these things would have happened.
If I hadn't gone to a party, I wouldn't have gone to bed late.
Make eight sentences.

Unit 38

A SATURDAY AFTERNOON

Laura felt slightly uneasy as the guard unlocked the gates and waved her through. The Blitzkopf Clinic was not an ordinary mental institution. It was the most exclusive institution of its type in the country. You had to be not only mentally ill, but also extremely wealthy to be accepted as a patient. She parked her car outside the main entrance of the sterile white main building. She paused on the steps to look at the beautiful flower gardens and surrounding grounds. An old man in a white straw hat was watering the flower bed beside the steps. He smiled at her.

Old man: Good afternoon. Pretty day, isn't it?
Laura: Yes, it certainly is.
Old man: Are you a new patient?
Laura: Oh, I'm not a patient. I'm just here to do some research.
Old man: Will you be staying long?
Laura: I really don't know. I wonder if you could tell me the way to Dr. Blitzkopf's office?
Old man: Certainly. Just go through the main door, turn left, walk down to the end of the hall, and it's the last door on the right.
Laura: Thank you very much.

Dr. Blitzkopf was expecting her. He had been looking forward to meeting his new research assistant. He himself had always been interested in the special problems of long-term patients. Dr. Blitzkopf was very proud of his clinic, and Laura was impressed by the relaxed and informal atmosphere. She spent the mornings interviewing patients and the afternoons in the flower gardens, writing up the results of her research. Some of the patients were withdrawn and depressed; some seemed almost normal. Only one or two had to be kept locked up. She found it hard to believe that all of them had been considered too dangerous to live in normal society. She often saw the old man in the straw hat. He spent most of his time working in the flower gardens, but he always stopped to speak to her. She found out that his name was Edward Beale. He was a gentle and mild-mannered old fellow, with clear, blue, honest eyes, white

hair, and a pinkish complexion. He always looked pleased with life. She became particularly curious about him, but Dr. Blitzkopf had never asked her to interview him, and she wondered why. One night, at dinner, she asked about Mr. Beale.

Dr. Blitzkopf: Ah, yes, Edward. Nice old guy. He's been here longer than anybody.
Laura: What's wrong with him?
Dr. Blitzkopf: Nothing. His family put him here thirty-five years ago. They never come to visit him, but the bills are always paid on time.
Laura: But what had he done?
Dr. Blitzkopf: I'll show you his file. It seems that he burned down his school when he was seventeen. His family tried to keep the incident quiet. Over the next few years there were a number of mysterious fires in his neighborhood, but the family did nothing until he tried to set fire to the family mansion. He was in here the next day. Edward never protested.

Laura: And that was thirty-five years ago!
Dr. Blitzkopf: I'm afraid so. If I'd had my way, I'd have let him out years ago.
Laura: But he couldn't still be dangerous!
Dr. Blitzkopf: No. He's had plenty of opportunities. We even let him smoke. If he'd wanted to start a fire, he could have done it at any time.

Laura was shocked by the story. She became determined to do something about it. She wrote letters to Edward's family, but never received a reply. He had never been officially certified as insane, and legally he could leave at any time. Dr. Blitzkopf was easily persuaded to let her talk to Edward.

Laura: Edward, have you ever thought about leaving this place?
Edward: No. I'm very happy here. This is my home. And anyway, I have nowhere else to go.
Laura: But wouldn't you like to go into town sometimes—to buy your own cigarettes?
Edward: I've never thought about it. I suppose it would be nice. But I wouldn't want to stay away for long. I've spent twenty years working on this garden. I know every flower and tree. What would happen to them if I weren't here?

Laura realized that it would be unkind to make him leave the hospital. However, she found out that the next Saturday was his birthday. She arranged with the staff to give him a party. They wanted it to be a surprise, and Dr. Blitzkopf agreed to let him go out for the afternoon. There was a flower show in town. Edward left at 2 o'clock. He seemed quite excited. They expected him to return about four o'clock. The cook had made a birthday cake, and the staff had decorated the lounge.

Laura was standing in the window when she saw him. He was early. He was walking up the drive toward the house, whistling cheerfully. Behind him, above the trees, thick black columns of smoke were beginning to rise slowly into the clear blue sky.

HOLIDAY USA

Can you see yourself riding a cable car in San Francisco, eating fresh crab at Fisherman's Wharf, winning a fortune in the casinos of Las Vegas, and walking with the stars along Hollywood Boulevard? TransAtlantic Airways invites you to spend two unforgettable weeks in California and Nevada and enjoy the glitter and the glamour of the Golden West.

Every city has its own character—San Francisco with the Golden Gate Bridge, Chinatown, Japantown, cable cars climbing up the steep hills, restaurants serving food from every country in the world. You'll go on tours to see the scenery of Monterey and Carmel and the breathtaking views from the Pacific Coast Highway.

Then you join in the excitement of Las Vegas, the gambling capital of the world, set in the Nevada Desert. Las Vegas never sleeps and the entertainment is the finest in the world. And from Las Vegas there's an optional flight over the spectacular Grand Canyon.

Finally you arrive in Los Angeles, home of the movie industry. Sunset Boulevard, Beverly Hills, and Hollywood all wait to welcome you. You'll be able to choose any number of tours—the wonderful world of Disneyland, Universal Studios, or even a shopping spree on Rodeo Drive.

This exciting three-city tour offers you a golden opportunity to experience the special atmosphere of the Golden West.

Matilda is Colombian and married to George Marek, an American teaching in Colombia. They've just returned to Colombia and Matilda is telling her friends about her first trip to the States.

"On the whole I enjoyed it very much, but it was pretty tiring. We went on most of the tours because I didn't want to miss anything. I really felt we needed more time. If I went again, I'd stay longer. I would have spent more time in San Francisco and less time in Los Angeles if I'd known more about the cities. Los Angeles was a little disappointing. We went on a tour of Beverly Hills to see the houses of the stars. But unless you had studied film history, you would never have heard of most of them! Generally speaking, the hotels, food, and service were excellent. And I found Californians particularly friendly. I probably took too much luggage. Clothes in California were so cheap! It would have been a good idea to take along an empty suitcase! If I'd done that, the savings on clothes would almost have paid for half of the air fare! Well, not really . . ."

The Rizzos, a retired couple from Damariscotta, Maine, were on the tour with the Mareks. Jack Rizzo was asked about the trip.

"We'd been looking forward to this trip for years, and it was the vacation of a lifetime. I think we enjoyed Las Vegas the most, but two nights were probably enough! If we'd stayed there much longer, we'd have lost all our money! We saw Dolly Parton at the Desert Inn. I've never seen anything like that place! Disneyland is a 'must' for anyone with children. If only we'd had our grandchildren with us! They would have loved it! We went on some of the tours, and we could have gone on more, but you can't see everything, can you? I didn't think much of the food there, but California wine was a nice surprise. We wouldn't have gone on this trip unless it had been an escorted tour group. We're not as young as we used to be, and we couldn't have done it on our own. Everyone, however, was so helpful to us."

Unit 40

HOLIDAY USA

Fly-Drive means freedom—the freedom of the road to explore this exciting country. Fly-Drive must be the logical way of seeing the Northeast. Get to your first destination by plane and then rent a comfortable car. It allows you the luxury of a flexible schedule—the ideal way of getting the most out of your vacation. We'll make a reservation at a wonderful hotel for your first night and your car will be delivered to you in the morning. Then you are as free as a bird to go and stay anywhere you'd like to. Or you can plan your driving route beforehand and we'll make all of your motel reservations for you in advance. When you prepay, we'll send you all of your motel confirmations, and your room will be waiting for you at each stop.

Boston is the ideal starting point for exploring New England. To the southeast are the rocky cliffs and sandy beaches of beautiful Cape Cod, ideal for swimming, sailing, and fishing. To the north is New Hampshire with its green valleys, lovely steepled churches, and infinite varieties of wildflowers. Drive up into Maine, a land of forests and mountains. Try the lobster in the charming restaurants along the spectacular coastline. Drive west across New York State to Niagara Falls or south through the beautiful rolling hills of Connecticut to a coastline of resort towns and fishing ports.

Luis and Carmen Noguera and their two children flew from Albuquerque, New Mexico to Boston to take the fly-drive vacation. Now Carmen is talking about it.

"We'd never have gone on a fly-drive vacation unless we'd had the kids with us. I think it's the only way to travel with young children. The distances were much greater than we had imagined. If we ever went East on vacation again, we wouldn't try to drive so far. I think we'd cover the longer distances by plane, and then rent a different car in each place. Of course, that gets expensive. We stayed at lovely, quaint country inns, which were perfect for all of us. They weren't too expensive, and the children were always made welcome. In fact, a few of the innkeepers offered to babysit. For us that was marvelous. We wouldn't have been able to leave the children if they hadn't offered. We would never have left them alone for too long, of course, but it was nice for us to get away from them for a few hours. New England was absolutely fantastic and we'd recommend it to anyone, especially in the fall."

Stephanie and Melissa Gold also took the fly-drive vacation from San Diego to visit their grandmother in Hanover, New Hampshire. Melissa spoke about their vacation.

"It was really great. After we visited our grandmother we explored New England. We took turns driving, so the distances didn't seem so long. One night we couldn't find a motel, but it was O.K. because we had rented a 1984 Cutlass Supreme. There was plenty of room to sleep! We bought lots of maple syrup. If we'd bought it in California, it would have cost almost three times as much. We took our vacation in the fall, so the colors of the trees in New England were unbelievable! We wouldn't have chosen this vacation plan unless we'd liked driving. You spend a lot of time in the car. We plan to go to the East Coast again next year, but we'll visit our other grandmother in Miami, if we can afford it."

Unit 40

FOOD FOR THOUGHT

"One man's meat is another man's poison."

Traditional proverb

There is a wide range of nutritious foods in the world. However, eating habits differ from country to country. In some societies certain foods are taboo. An eccentric millionaire once invited guests from several countries to a banquet and offered them this menu. All the foods are popular in some parts of the world, but are not eaten in others.

Appetizers

Snails
Frogs' legs
Pigs' feet
Oysters
Caviar
100-year-old eggs
Tripe (cow's stomach)
Blood sausage
Live sea urchins

Soups

Bird's nest soup
Shark fin soup
Seaweed soup

Fish

Octopus
Jellied eels

Main Courses

Cow brains
Whole stuffed camel
Grilled songbirds
Roast snake
Bat stew
Horsemeat
Kangaroo
Whale
Roast dog
Pork
Beef
Lamb
Veal
Alligator steak

Dessert

Chocolate-covered ants
Salad of flower petals

If you had been there, which items could you have eaten? Which items would you have eaten? Which items couldn't you have eaten? Why not?

Do you know which countries they are popular in? Would you eat them if you were starving?

What unusual things are eaten in your country? Does your country/region/state have a national/regional dish? How do you make it?

"Part of the secret of success in life is to eat what you like, and let the food fight it out inside you."

Mark Twain

Here are some common ideas about food: Eating carrots is good for the eyes.
Fish is good for the brain.
Eating cheese at night makes you dream.
Garlic keeps you from getting colds.
Drinking coffee keeps you from sleeping.
Yogurt makes you live long.
An apple a day keeps the doctor away.
Warm milk helps you go to sleep.
A cup of tea settles your stomach.
Brown eggs taste better than white ones.

Have you heard similar expressions? Do you agree or disagree with them?

"More die in the United States of too much food than too little."

John Kenneth Galbraith

At different times in different countries there have been different ideas of beauty. The rich would always want to look fat in a society where food was scarce and to look thin in a society where food was plentiful. The current interest in losing weight is because of fashion as well as health. However, overeating causes a variety of illnesses.

Do you know what they are? Are you overweight/average/underweight? Does it bother you? Have you ever been on a diet? What did you eat? What foods should you eat/not eat if you want to lose weight? What should you eat if you want to put on weight?

"One should eat to live, not live to eat."

Molière

" ... set yourself at a restaurant in front of an eight-ounce steak and then imagine the room filled with 45 to 50 people with empty bowls in front of them. For the 'feed cost' of your steak, each of their bowls could be filled with a full cup of cooked cereal grains!"

Frances Moore Lappé, Diet for a Small Planet

"Year by year, while the world's population has increased, the food supply has increased more. (But) ... supplies of nourishing food could be enormously increased if, in the richer countries of the world, people were prepared to eat some of the food they feed to their pigs and cattle ... and to their pet dogs and cats."

Dr. Magnus Pyke

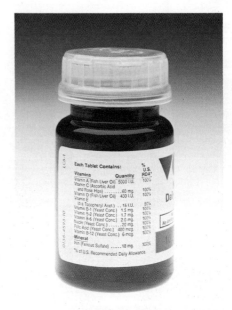

I WISH...

Lawrence B. Waspasson: Yes?

Judy: Your call from New York's on line one. Paris has just come through on line two, and there's a call from Tokyo on line four.

L. B. Waspasson: Ask them to call back tomorrow, Judy. Tell them . . . tell them I'm not here. It's too late. I wish I wasn't here. I've had enough today.

Judy: But they're urgent, all of them.

L. B. Waspasson: Do you know something, Judy? I wish I was at home now, in front of the television with a cup of hot chocolate.

Paul: Look at that! It's pouring rain again, and I have to walk to the bus stop.

Diane: Well, at least it's not snow.

Paul: It's all right for Waspasson. His Cadillac is downstairs waiting to take him home.

Diane: Yeah. I wish I had a chauffeur-driven limousine.

Paul: I wish I had a car, any car. I'm going to get soaked tonight!

Tony: Hi, Jane. Still here?

Jane: Yes. I'm waiting to see Waspasson.

Tony: You don't usually work late.

Jane: I wish I wasn't working this evening. There's a good game on TV.

Tony: Oh well. Maybe he'll call you in soon.

Jane: I hope he does!

Alan: Haven't you left yet?

Lorraine: No. I wish I had. I can't go until I've finished this report.

Alan: Can't you do it tomorrow?

Lorraine: I wish I could, but Waspasson wants it tonight.

Shirley: How are you doing, Joe?

Joe: Oh hi, Shirley. I don't feel like working tonight.

Shirley: Neither do I. I hate this kind of work.

Joe: Why do you do it then?

Shirley: I wish I didn't have to! But we need the money. My husband's out of work again.

Joe: I know what you mean. I wish I'd learned how to type, or something like that.

Shirley: We can all wish! I dropped out of school at sixteen. I wish I hadn't, but I never got good grades and I hated it. Kids have it really easy in school nowadays. I wish we'd had a better chance. I'd never have ended up cleaning offices.

Joe: Come on, Shirley, let's try to finish early and go to a movie.

Police Officer: Look at that, Sergeant. There are still lights on in the insurance company again.

Sergeant: Yes, it looks nice and warm, doesn't it? I sometimes wish I worked there.

P.O.: You do? Really?

Sergeant: Uh huh. Sometimes. A nice office, a desk, secretaries everywhere. It can't be bad.

P.O.: And the boss's Caddy outside.

Sergeant: Still, you know what they say: "the grass is always greener on the other side."

P.O.: I suppose you're right, Sarge. Hey, that Cadillac is in front of a fire hydrant.

Sergeant: Oh, yeah. Give him a parking ticket, Lucy. He can afford it!

Exercise 1

1. I wish I was on vacation.
   I wish I was in Hawaii.
   Where do you wish you were now?
   Do you wish you were in bed?/at home?/on the beach?
2. I'm a student.
   I wish I was an actor.
   What do you wish you were?

Exercise 2

I don't have a car. *I wish I had a car.*
Make five sentences.

Exercise 3

It's raining.
I wish it wasn't raining.
She's working.
She wishes she wasn't working.
Continue.
1. The phones are ringing.
2. It's snowing.
3. She's sitting in an office.
4. He's waiting.

Exercise 4

She hasn't finished yet.
She wishes she had finished.
I didn't learn how to type.
I wish I had learned how to type.
Continue.
1. They haven't done their homework.
2. She dropped out of school at sixteen.
3. I haven't seen that movie.
4. He lost his wallet.

THE HAPPIEST DAYS OF YOUR LIFE?

Some people say that your days in school are the happiest days of your life. Here are five people talking about their experiences.

Kaye Wilson works in an advertising agency.

"I went to a big public high school in the Midwest. We lived in a well-to-do suburb, so the school was pretty good academically. I'm sorry I didn't take more advantage of it. I wish my parents had let me take more science and math subjects. No, I wish I had insisted on taking what I wanted to. For college they sent me East to a fancy girls' school so that I could marry some boy from Harvard or Yale or one of those places. For them, girls went to college only to meet the 'right boy' and, as a second thought, to 'have something to fall back on' in case your husband died, and you had to go to work. I thought they were right and I was wrong, so I majored in literature. It was so boring! I finally got through the four years, but I never met the 'right boy.' Instead of 'falling back' on teaching literature, I'm in advertising and the vice-president of this agency. It's O.K., but if I had taken the subjects I wanted, I would be an engineer or . . . an astronaut. I wish my teachers had given me better advice. I'm really sorry they didn't tell me I wasn't crazy."

Wade Hamlin is a successful self-employed builder.

"School? It's a waste of time mostly—at least it was for me. I quit after my sophomore year in college because I stopped hoping that I would ever learn anything. I wanted to start earning a living—in the real world. The biggest problem with school is the teachers. Most of them are bored with their jobs, so they're boring in their classes. That old saying is really right: Those who can't do anything, teach. Teachers are overpaid, and their vacations are too long. I don't know what they're always complaining about. They can't even teach kids today to read and write. If I had listened to my teachers, I would know all about Shakespeare and what day the Civil War started and how to conjugate Spanish verbs and how to prove the Pythagorean Theorem and all that

junk. But I wouldn't know anything about how to make a business deal or raise my kids or anything that's really important. I'm sorry I went to school at all."

Anne Marie Carpenter is the personnel manager of a department store.

"I loved school. All my teachers were wonderful; I learned something special from each one. I was a straight A student almost every year, but I didn't spend all my time studying. I participated in a lot of extra-curricular activities and sports too. I was in student government both in high school and in college. I was always sorry when summer vacation started—three months with no school! Most kids liked vacations more than school, but not me. Some of my friends in high school didn't go to college, but they regret it now. Some of them would have done well if they had been encouraged to go. I only regret not going to graduate school after I got my bachelor's degree. I've started an MBA at night, but it's not the same. Work is all right, but I miss the friends and the fun that went along with the studying."

Craig Phillips is a Wall Street stock broker.

"I went to a prep school in Connecticut, and then I went to Harvard. I guess you could say I had the best education money could buy, but it wasn't easy. We had to study very hard, and a lot was expected of us. The thing I remember most is the friendships. The friends I made then are still my friends today. Most of us were together in prep school and then at Harvard too. Sports were very important for me. I believe that team sports teach people to work together, and competition with another team brings out the best in people. 'It's not winning or losing, but how you play the game that counts.' Anyway, discipline was stricter then. It's too bad that has changed. Maybe young people would be better behaved nowadays if there were more discipline in the schools. My biggest regret is that I didn't have the family life other boys had. After age twelve I only saw my family at Christmas and in the summer, when I would go home to Cleveland. I've

thought about that problem but I still want my children to go to boarding schools in New England. It'll do them good."

Coleen McGrath is a factory worker.

"School was just another part of neighborhood life. My brothers and sisters and I went to a parochial elementary school three blocks from home. Later we had to take a bus to the public high school, but it was only a 10-minute ride. And then we all went to a little community college. I wish my kids could do that. I have to take the youngest in the car to the big elementary school over across the river. A school bus picks up the other two who are in junior high school, and it takes them almost an hour each way. I wish things hadn't changed so much."

Schools in the United States:

Elementary school: Kindergarten and Grades 1 to 6.
Junior High (or Middle) School: Grades 7 and 8 or 7 to 9.
(Senior) High School: Grades 10 to 12 or 9 to 12.
Community Colleges: Usually 2-year degree and extension programs.
College: Four-year bachelor's degree programs, usually liberal arts.
University: Four-year bachelor's and undergraduate professional degree colleges; graduate degree (masters and doctorate) programs.

Special Terms:

Parochial schools provide general education along with religious training, usually Roman Catholic.
Prep schools are private college-preparatory high schools.
Note: Almost all schools, colleges, etc., are now coeducational (that is, with both male and female students).

Exercise

What about your days in school?
What do/did you like?
What don't/didn't you like?
What about sports?/discipline?/subjects you liked/didn't like?/teachers?/extra-curricular activities?

MISS AMERICA

Ron Parks: We have come to the end of an exciting week here in Atlantic City, New Jersey, and we are ready to crown the new Miss America. We have seen the contestants in bathing suits and evening gowns. And we have watched our semi-finalists perform in the talent portion of the contest. In addition, all 50 contestants were interviewed by the judges at the beginning of the week. So in addition to beauty and talent, the contestants are judged on charm, intelligence, and personality.

Now listen to the interviews with the five finalists and complete the blue chart at the bottom of the page.

Exercise

Ask and answer questions about each of the finalists: What state is she from? How old is she? What school does she go to? What are her hobbies? What's her ambition? If she could have one wish, what would she wish for?

If you were a judge, which contestant would you choose, and why? Listen to the results, and complete this chart:

Winners	Name	Scholarships
4th runner-up		
3rd runner-up		
2nd runner-up		
1st runner-up		
MISS AMERICA		

Beauty Pageants—Points of View:

"I never watch beauty pageants. They're like a cattle market! I think they insult the intelligence of women. No woman with any self-respect would ever enter a contest like this. I find them totally degrading!"

"I certainly don't take them too seriously. They're really harmless fun. I mean, you see prettier girls every day in stores and offices. But if people earn a living from their intelligence, why shouldn't they make money from their appearance?"

"I occasionally watch them, but I don't think I'd like them if I were a woman. After all, a lot of girls would look just as good with the make-up, clothes, and lights. Anyway, beauty's only skin deep. I often feel annoyed when I'm watching a beauty pageant. The values are false."

"I always watch them. I enjoy looking at pretty girls. I'd rather watch a beauty pageant then a depressing program about politics. There isn't enough glamour in the world. If you don't like it, you can always turn off the TV."

Contestant	State	Age	School	Hobbies	Ambition	Wish
Rita Rae Simpson	Florida	18	University of Miami	sewing cooking	to work with children	a large family
LaDonna Lincoln						
Amy Lou Peterson						
Lucia Delgado						
Susan Lee Jamison						

OPERATION IMPOSSIBLE

Unit 45

T: Well, 006, I'm happy that M let you come to Washington to work with us on this operation.

006: We're always happy to cooperate, sir.

T: Now, 006. I want you to look at these pictures carefully. This could be the most important mission of your life. At last we have the chance to break the biggest crime syndicate in the world—SMASH. Look at the man on the right. He's the one we've been after for years.

006: Who is he?

T: We think he's the one that controls SMASH. He's certainly the one that ordered the murder of 003, the one that planned the hijacking of the jumbo jet full of world leaders, and he organizes the biggest drug-smuggling operation in the world.

006: Do we know his name?

T: We know some of them. Otto Krugerand, that's the name he uses in legitimate business. Dr. Nada, that's the name he was using in Vienna last year. John Smith, that's the signature he left on a hotel register in Hong Kong.

006: Who's the gorilla standing behind him?

T: Ah, Slojob. He's the bodyguard who travels everywhere with Krugerand, and the only person he trusts. He's an expert assassin. He's the one who fed 004 to the alligators.

006: How charming! What about the woman?

T: Don't you recognize her?

006: No, I've never seen her before.

T: You would have recognized her, if she hadn't had plastic surgery and dyed her hair. Think back to Singapore.

006: Not Mala Powers! She's the one who arranged the pipeline explosion and then vanished into thin air!

T: She's also Krugerand's wife and the only pilot he allows to fly his private plane.

006: Who's the little guy wearing thick glasses?

T: That's Professor Peratoff, the mad scientist who defected from Moldania. He's an expert on laser technology and the first man who's been able to perfect a space laser weapon. Krugerand is planning to build a private space rocket which could put a satellite into orbit. Do you understand the importance of this, 006? If they got a laser weapon into space, they could blackmail the world. That's something which must not happen, 006!

T: Take a look at this picture, 006.

006: It's an oil rig.

T: It looks like it, doesn't it? It belongs to Krugerand's oil company. It's a rig that's supposed to be drilling for oil in the Indian Ocean. Below it, there's a vast underwater complex.

006: The superstructure looks odd.

T: In fact it conceals the launching pad they're going to use for the rocket.

006: That must be a radar scanner, there.

T: Yes. It's the scanner they'll use to track the rocket, but they can also see anything that tries to get near the rig. It's going to be very difficult to get you in, 006.

006: There's a helicopter pad.

T: We think that would be too dangerous. Look at the helicopter closely. It carries air-to-air missiles which could destroy any aircraft approaching the rig.

006: How are we going to do it then?

T: We're flying you to California tonight for two weeks of intensive mini-submarine training.

006: That sounds like fun!

T: And 006, try not to be late for the plane. M has told me about you.

006: Oh, he has? Don't worry, sir. I'll be on time.

Exercise 1

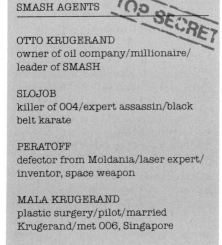

```
SMASH AGENTS        TOP SECRET

OTTO KRUGERAND
owner of oil company/millionaire/
leader of SMASH

SLOJOB
killer of 004/expert assassin/black
belt karate

PERATOFF
defector from Moldania/laser expert/
inventor, space weapon

MALA KRUGERAND
plastic surgery/pilot/married
Krugerand/met 006, Singapore
```

Krugerand.

He's the one	*who*	*owns an oil company.*
	that	
He's the one	*who*	*'s a millionaire.*
	that	

Make more sentences like this.

Exercise 2

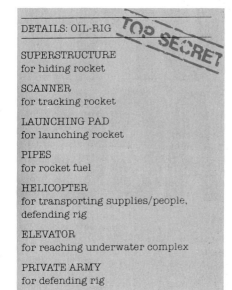

```
DETAILS: OIL-RIG          TOP SECRET

SUPERSTRUCTURE
for hiding rocket

SCANNER
for tracking rocket

LAUNCHING PAD
for launching rocket

PIPES
for rocket fuel

HELICOPTER
for transporting supplies/people,
defending rig

ELEVATOR
for reaching underwater complex

PRIVATE ARMY
for defending rig
```

What's that?

| *It's the scanner* | *which* | *they'll use* |
| | *that* | *to track the rocket.* |

Make more sentences.

Exercise 3

She's the woman. He met her in Singapore.

She's the woman he met in Singapore.

Continue.

1. 003 was the agent. Slojob killed him.
2. Otto Krugerand's the leader. We've been trying to catch him.
3. Smith was the name. He used it in Hong Kong.
4. Mala Power's the woman. Otto Krugerand married her.
5. Peratoff is the scientist. SMASH recruited him.
6. They're the people. 006 must stop them.

OPERATION ACCOMPLISHED

Exercise 1
Look at the itinerary on the opposite page.
He went to California where he learned to handle a mini-sub.
He went back to Washington where he was given a transmitter.
He was given a transmitter, which was put into the heel of his shoe.
Make complete sentences, using "where" and "which" about 006's itinerary.

When 006 reached the rig he climbed up one of the towers. He was looking for someone whose uniform he could steal, but the rig seemed deserted. He went into an empty cabin. As he was looking for a change of clothes, the guard, whose cabin he was searching, came in. He was surprised to see 006 in his black frogman's suit, and 006 had no difficulty in silencing him with one blow to the neck. Fortunately the guard was about the same size as 006, and the uniform fit perfectly. There was a pass in the pocket. The pass operated the elevator which went down to the underwater complex.

Exercise 2
Look at the diagram on the opposite page.
★*This is where 006 left the mini-sub.*
Look at the diagram, and make ten more sentences like this.

006 woke up with his hands tied behind his back. His head was throbbing. He was not alone. In the room were Otto Krugerand, Slojob, Mala, and the guard whose clothes he was wearing. And a beautiful woman, whose hands were also tied, was lying beside him. 006 recognized her instantly. She was Pic Welles, an American agent he'd met in Washington. 006 looked at his watch. The explosive device he'd put on the rig was timed

to explode in 45 minutes. Otto noticed that 006 was awake.

"Welcome, Commander Fleming. We've been expecting you," he said smiling. "Unfortunately we don't have time to show you around. Blast-off is in forty minutes. Slojob will take you to feed the sharks. They must be very hungry by now."

"I'm delighted to meet you, Krugerand. I've been looking forward to it. Thank you for your invitation. I've always been interested in big fish. See you later."

"I don't think so, Commander. This will be your last mission. Slojob! Take Commander Fleming and Miss Welles to the aquarium."

Slojob escorted them to the Krugerand's private apartment. One wall was made of thick glass and behind it 006 could see the dark shapes of the sharks, swimming around. Slojob pushed them up a spiral staircase to a platform above the shark tank.

"Ladies first," 006 said politely.

"No, no. After you," replied Pic Welles with a smile on her face.

"You wouldn't refuse us a last cigarette, would you, Slojob?" 006 asked.

"I don't smoke," Slojob grinned. "And you should give up smoking, it's bad for your health."

"Now, come on, Slojob. There are some cigarettes and a lighter in my pocket." 006 indicated his jacket pocket.

"O.K. But don't try anything." Slojob reached into 006's pocket and took out the cigarettes and lighter. He was careful to keep his gun trained on 006 all the time. He took a cigarette out of the pack and pushed it into 006's mouth. He pressed the lighter with his thumb. The sudden force of the flame took him by surprise. At that moment 006 kicked him in the stomach. He fell backwards and disappeared into the tank. Within seconds all that re-

mained of him was a red pool of blood on the surface.

The lighter had dropped to the floor and was still burning, and 006 was able to burn through the ropes which held his hands. He quickly released Pic. He glanced at his watch.

"We don't have much time," he said. "Can you fly a helicopter?"

"What I don't know I'll learn quickly," she replied calmly.

"Good. Go and get the engines started and be ready to go. If I'm not there in exactly ten minutes, go without me."

006 ran back to the control room and walked calmly in. "Good evening," he said. Otto turned, and he was moving his hand towards his pocket when a jet of flame from 006's lighter threw him back across the room. 006 pointed the lighter at Peratoff and Mala while he pulled every switch on the control panel until it exploded and burst into flames. 006 ran quickly to the elevator, but it was on fire. He had five minutes left, and he started to climb the ladder in the elevator shaft. He was halfway up when he felt a hand grabbing at his ankles. It was Otto! 006 gripped the ladder tightly, turned and kicked him hard in the face. He fell back, screaming, into the flames below. The helicopter was already in the air, hovering about 3 feet above the pad. 006 leapt onto a landing skid, shouting, "Take it up! Take it up!" The helicopter soared into the sky. A few seconds later there was a massive explosion as the rig went up. 006 managed to climb into the helicopter cabin. He sat back, reached into his pocket, and took out his cigarettes. He put one in his mouth. "Oh blast!" he said. "I seem to have forgotten my lighter. You don't have a light, do you?"

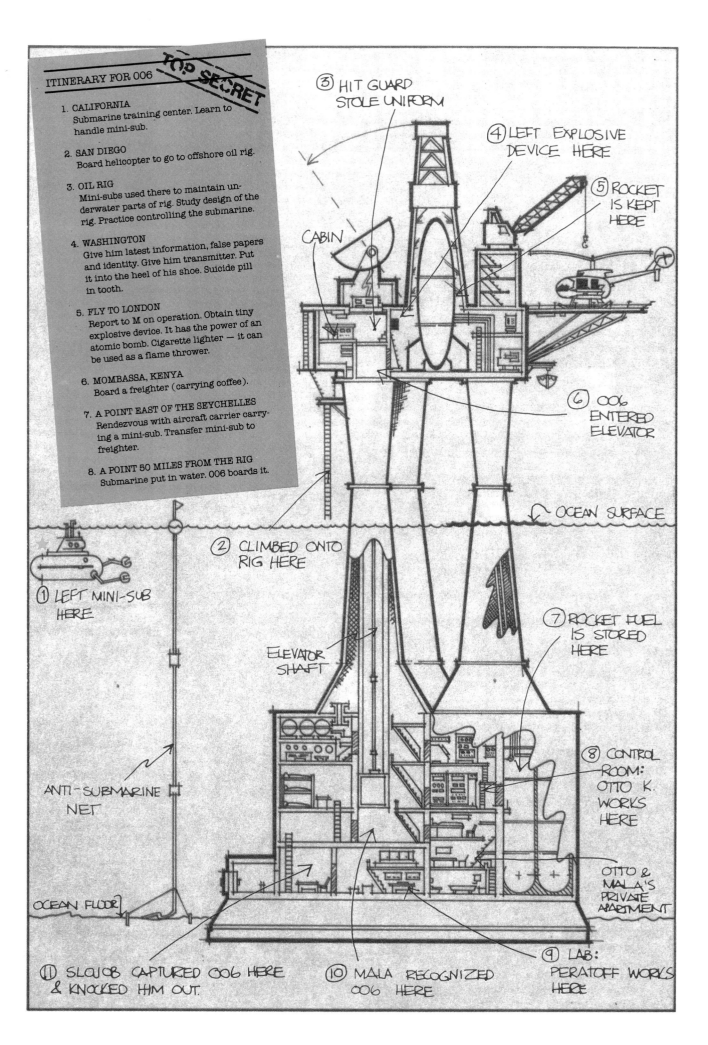

ITINERARY FOR 006

~~TOP SECRET~~

1. CALIFORNIA
   Submarine training center. Learn to handle mini-sub.

2. SAN DIEGO
   Board helicopter to go to offshore oil rig.

3. OIL RIG
   Mini-subs used there to maintain underwater parts of rig. Study design of the rig. Practice controlling the submarine.

4. WASHINGTON
   Give him latest information, false papers and identity. Give him transmitter. Put it into the heel of his shoe. Suicide pill in tooth.

5. FLY TO LONDON
   Report to M on operation. Obtain tiny explosive device. It has the power of an atomic bomb. Cigarette lighter — it can be used as a flame thrower.

6. MOMBASSA, KENYA
   Board a freighter (carrying coffee).

7. A POINT EAST OF THE SEYCHELLES
   Rendezvous with aircraft carrier carrying a mini-sub. Transfer mini-sub to freighter.

8. A POINT 50 MILES FROM THE RIG
   Submarine put in water. 006 boards it.

③ HIT GUARD STOLE UNIFORM

④ LEFT EXPLOSIVE DEVICE HERE

⑤ ROCKET IS KEPT HERE

CABIN

⑥ 006 ENTERED ELEVATOR

OCEAN SURFACE

① LEFT MINI-SUB HERE

② CLIMBED ONTO RIG HERE

⑦ ROCKET FUEL IS STORED HERE

ELEVATOR SHAFT

⑧ CONTROL ROOM: OTTO K. WORKS HERE

ANTI-SUBMARINE NET

OTTO & MALA'S PRIVATE APARTMENT

OCEAN FLOOR

⑪ SLOJOB CAPTURED 006 HERE & KNOCKED HIM OUT.

⑩ MALA RECOGNIZED 006 HERE

⑨ LAB: PERATOFF WORKS HERE

STUDENT MASTERMIND

Host: Our next contestant on "Student Mastermind" is Vickie McLean, who is a student at Portstown High School. Let me just remind you of the rules, Vickie. You have two minutes in which to answer as many questions as possible. If you do not know the answer, you should say, "Pass." I will then go on to the next question. If you answer incorrectly, I will then give the correct answer. You will get one point for each correct answer. If two contestants have the same number of points at the end, the one who has the fewest number of passes will be the winner. Are you ready?

Vickie: Yes.

Host: Can you name the President of the United States whose early career began as a radio sports announcer?

Vickie: Uh—Reagan. Ronald Reagan.

Host: Correct. What is an instrument which shows the direction of north?

Vickie: A compass?

Host: Correct. Can you tell me the name of the sea where eels go to spawn and die?

Vickie: Uh . . . hmm . . . pass.

Host: Name the person who became the first woman prime minister of India.

Vickie: Mrs. Gandhi. Indira Gandhi.

Host: Exactly. What is the date when France celebrates their revolution of 1789?

Vickie: The fourteenth of July.

Host: Correct. What do we call a person who always expects the best to happen?

Vickie: Uh—an optimist.

Host: Correct. Can you tell me the language that was spoken in the Roman Empire?

Vickie: Italian?

Host: No, wrong. The correct answer is Latin. What kind of person do people visit when they want advice about their marriage?

Vickie: Pass.

Host: Who was the Egyptian queen whose beauty was famous throughout the world?

Vickie: Cleopatra.

Host: That's correct. What's the kind of school where very rich people send their children before college?

Vickie: Uh—private school?

Host: Can you be more exact?

Vickie: No. I can't think of it.

Host: I'm afraid I can't give you that. We were looking for "prep school" or "preparatory school." Now can you tell me . . . *(Ding)* I've started, so I'll finish. Can you tell me the

name of the French Emperor whose final battle was at Waterloo?

Vickie: Napoleon Bonaparte.

Host: Correct. And at the end of that round Vickie McLean has scored seven points. You passed on two. The sea where eels go to spawn and die is the Sargasso Sea, and the kind of person people visit when they want advice about their marriage is a "marriage counselor." Thank you. Can we have our next contestant, please?

Exercise 1

Now practice the game with a partner.

Questions

1. What's a person who breaks into a house and steals things?
2. Who was the boxer whose most famous words were "I am the greatest?"
3. What do we call a store where bread is made and sold?
4. What is the day when Christians celebrate the birth of Jesus?
5. What's the place where you go to wait for the announcement for a plane?
6. What's a tool which is used for digging?
7. Can you tell me the unusual system of public transportation which is used in San Francisco?
8. Can you name the American president who was assassinated in 1963?
9. What do Americans call a hotel which is especially for people traveling by car?
10. Name the two young lovers whose tragic story was made into a play by Shakespeare.

burglar / Muhammed Ali / bakery / Christmas Day / gate / shovel / cable car / John F. Kennedy / motel / Romeo and Juliet

Exercise 2

Work with a partner. One of you uses List A, the other uses List B. Each of you writes down ten questions using the words *who/which/where/when/whose* given in parentheses in the list. Your questions must give the answer provided in the list. For example:

Neil Armstrong (who)
Q: *Can you tell me the name of the first man who walked on the moon?*
A: *Neil Armstrong.*

widower (whose)
Q: *What do you call a man whose wife has died?*
A: *A widower.*

Now, with books closed, ask your partner the questions you have prepared. Your partner will then ask you to answer the questions he or she has prepared.

List A
Neil Armstrong (who)
sailor (who)
receipt (which)
submarine (which)
newstand (where)
casino (where)
golden wedding anniversary (when)
employment agency (when)
widow (whose)
Josephine Bonaparte (whose)

List B
widower (whose)
Columbus (who)
sleeping pill (which)
driver's license (which)
lost and found department (where)
silver wedding anniversary (when)
Yoko Ono (whose)
pilot (who)

THE MIDDLEBURG HERALD

Vol. LXVI No. 262   *Thursday, September 19, 1984*   *Price 30¢*

INSIDE

Wolfe Recaptured
Alan Wolfe, who again escaped from the Maryland penitentiary, has been recaptured. Page A6

New Construction
The construction industry, which is an important indicator of the economy's direction, reports fewer new buildings started in the last three months. Page D1

Willie fired
George Steinmetz, who is owner of the Los Angeles Dodgers, today fired Manager Willie Martin — again. Page B1

$2 Million Homer
A recently found painting, which experts refuse to attribute to Winslow Homer, was sold for a record $2 million by Northeby's. Page C2

Miles Drops Out
Tim Miles, the racing driver whose legs were badly injured in last year's Grand Prix accident, says he will never race again. Page B3

Calypso No. 1
Central Motors' Calypso, whose success has surprised CM officials as much as the competition, is now the best-selling car in the U.S. Page D2

MYSTERY EXPLOSION IN INDIAN OCEAN
Oil rig destroyed in blast

SEYCHELLES ISLANDS, Sept. 26 (PAI). An oil rig in the Indian Ocean, which is located about 200 miles from these islands, exploded mysteriously yesterday. The oil rig, which had been drilling a test well, belonged to the Krugerand Corporation. A series of bright flashes, which were observed by ships 60 miles away, preceded shock waves of unusual force. Several ships, which rushed to the rescue, have been searching for survivors, but so far none have been found. It is not known how many people were working on the rig at the time of the explosion. Krugerand Corp., which is based in Switzerland, would not com-
(continued on page A9)

DANIEL STRIKES CAROLINA COAST
Floods and Winds Cause Extensive Damage

CAPE HATTERAS, N.C., Sept. 26 (WP). Hurricane Daniel, which is this season's fourth hurricane, became the first to hit this coastal area in 20 years. Gale winds, which at times reached a force of 100 mph, downed power lines and destroyed beach houses. Flooding, which was caused by torrential rains and high waves, left highways and roads impassable through last night. Coastal residents, who had been evacuated to inland locations, waited for the flood waters to subside before they returned to their homes, which might have been damaged by the storm.

Governor Frank Scott called out the National Guard to help the Red Cross, which is working around the clock in the emergency. The Guard will also assist local efforts to reopen the area's streets and roads, which were blocked by fallen trees and other debris.

The Governor, who toured the hardest hit areas by helicopter, asked the Federal Government to declare the area a national disaster. The President, who is spending the weekend at Camp David, is expected to make the declaration today. The declaration, which will apply only to the hardest-hit areas on the coast, will make millions of Federal dollars available for emergency relief. The Governor has already announced emergency small-business loans, which will help supermarkets and other essential businesses make needed repairs.

Electrical repair personnel, who have worked long hours to restore electric service to the area, are being called the real heroes of this natural disaster. Even off-duty personnel and many on vacation went to work on the numerous downed power lines, which had left the area without electricity for up to twelve hours in some parts.

More photos and related articles on page A6

KIDNAPPED GIRL FOUND SAFE

COLLINGWOOD, PA., Sept. 26 (WP). Caroline Newton, who police have been looking for since last Monday, has been found safe and sound. Fourteen-year-old Caroline, whose parents are well-known and wealthy doctors, was found in a house in Bayside, only 20 miles from her home. Neighbors, who were suspicious of the new renters, called police. The alleged kidnappers, who were arrested and charged by police last night, rented the house under the name "Mr. and Mrs. Harry Gilmore" and
continued on page A6

SHERIDAN STREET HOLDOUT STANDS FIRM

Mayor Unable to Persuade Woman and Dogs to Move

MIDTONVILLE, Sept. 26 (PAI). Mrs. Florence Hamilton, who has gained national attention in her fight to remain in her home, is still refusing to move, and the "Battle of Sheridan Street" continues. Midtonville Mayor Eileen Cox, who had not taken part in the battle until today, joined Housing Authority Director Hilda Martinez in front of Mrs. Hamilton's house at 2:30 this afternoon.

The house, which the Housing Authority wants to demolish to make way for a large public housing development, now stands alone. The Mayor, who was elected on her promises to put people, and especially the poor, above other concerns, spoke to Mrs. Hamilton by bull-

horn, asking her to come out and meet with her. She was forced to retreat to her limousine, which stood at the curb, doors open, when Mrs. Hamilton answered by turning loose two of her dogs, the two who are now recognized by veteran "war correspondents" as Caesar and Nero.

Mrs. Hamilton, whose plight has inspired a wave of public support, repeated her refusals to move in an interview with reporters later. A group of teenagers, who used to be Mrs. Hamilton's neighbors, arrived with food for her and the dogs. They wore T-shirts with "HANG IN THERE, FLO" printed on the front.
continued on page A9

WONDER DRUG BANNED BY FDA

WASHINGTON, D.C., Sept. 26 (PAI). The so-called wonder drug "Kural," which some doctors have been recommending as a pain-killer, has been banned by the Federal Drug Administration. After extensive clinical tests, which were first demanded by Ralph Raider, the drug has been found to produce alarming side-effects in laboratory mice. A spokesperson for Kurex Pharmaceuticals, which produces "Kural," protested the FDA's decision but in a statement to the press indicated that all tablets now in stores will be recalled. The FDA ban stated that while "Kural" is certainly an effective pain-killer, the drug "speeds up the aging process, which leads to premature hair loss, stiffening of the joints, loss of memory, and, eventually, premature senility." The
continued on page D2

BUSINESS CORRESPONDENCE

1339 Elm Ave.
Memphis, TN 38104

July 20, 1984

Manager, Lighthouse Motel
675 Gulf Breeze Drive
Gulf Shores, AL 36143

Dear Manager:

I am writing in reference to some items of laundry which were lost and damaged during my last stay there. When my laundry was returned on June 15, which was the day I checked out, I found that two socks, one brown and one black, were missing. Also a shirt, which had been yellow, was a sickly green. The housekeeper, to whom I complained, assured me that the missing socks would be mailed to me along with a check for $20 to cover the cost of the shirt, which I had bought only a few days before.

More than a month has passed, and I have received nothing.

Thank you for your attention to this matter.

Sincerely yours,

Charles Gardner
Charles Gardner

Lighthouse Motel · 675 Gulf Breeze Drive · Gulf Shores, AL 36143 · (205) 387-4141

August 15, 1984

Mr. Charles Gardner
1339 Elm Ave.
Memphis, TN 38104

Dear Mr. Gardner:

Thank you for your letter of July 20 in which you ask about missing and damaged items in your laundry while staying at our motel.

We regret that we are unable to trace the items to which you refer. The housekeeper to whom you spoke is no longer with us. May we remind you that the form on which you listed your laundry states very clearly that the motel is not responsible for loss or damage. The plastic bag in which you placed your clothes has the same warning printed in large letters on it.

We apologize for your inconvenience and hope that you will be staying with us again in the near future.

Sincerely yours,

Angela Martin
Angela Martin

1339 Elm Ave.
Memphis, TN 38104

August 28, 1984

Ms. Gloria Navarro
Proprietor, Lighthouse Motel
675 Gulf Breeze Drive
Gulf Shores, AL 36143

Dear Ms. Navarro:

Enclosed please find a copy of your manager's reply to a recent letter of mine, a copy of which is also enclosed. I am hoping that you will remember that we met one day by the motel pool and that you will ask the manager to reconsider her unhelpful attitude.

Thank you for your kindness.

Sincerely yours,

Charles Gardner
Charles Gardner

Lighthouse Motel · 675 Gulf Breeze Drive · Gulf Shores, AL 36143 · (205) 387-4141

September 29, 1984

Mr. Charles Gardner
1339 Elm Ave.
Memphis, TN 38104

Dear Mr. Gardner:

Thank you for your letter of August 28 to Ms. Gloria Navarro, for whom I am handling all correspondence during her absence. Ms. Navarro is on an extended trip abroad. She instructed me to refer all motel matters to the new manager, Harold Chester, to whom I have passed your letter.

Sincerely yours,

Greg Larkin
Greg Larkin
for Gloria Navarro

---

412 Leola Street
Albuquerque, NM 87131

February 2, 1984

Pears Lowbuck Co.
2882 Huron Street
Chicago, IL 60606

Dear Sir or Madam:

On January 10 I bought an acrylic turtleneck sweater from your store in the Eastdale Mall in Albuquerque. I had worn the sweater only twice when I discovered a hole in the left sleeve. I took the sweater back to the store. The salesclerk from whom I had bought the sweater and the manager, to whom I spoke later, both refused to exchange it or to refund my money. I cannot accept that; I am, therefore, writing to you in hopes of a more satisfactory solution.

Under separate cover I am sending you the sweater in question as well as a photocopy of my receipt which clearly shows the price and the date on which it was purchased. I should add that I have bought several Pears sweaters recently, all of which have developed holes in the sleeves.

I look forward to hearing from you on this matter.

Sincerely yours,

Roberta G. Tallchief
Roberta G. Tallchief

 Pears Lowbuck & Co.
2882 Huron Street, Chicago, IL 60606

March 15, 1984

Ms. Roberta G. Tallchief
412 Leola Street
Albuquerque, NM 87131

Dear Ms. Tallchief:

Please find in the mailer to which this letter is attached the sweater which you sent us on February 2. The salesclerk and manager in Albuquerque, to whom you first complained, were correct in refusing to exchange the sweater or refund your money. All Pears Lowbuck products are inspected before they leave the factory at which they are produced, and we guarantee their quality. This guarantee, however, covers only normal use. The sweater about which you wrote to complain has been subjected to unusual stress according to our Quality Control Department.

We appreciate the opportunity to clarify this matter. Leather elbow patches would probably prevent future problems with your sweaters. These patches, which can be applied with a hot iron, are available at the Pears Lowbuck store nearest you.

Sincerely yours,

Tanya Byrne

WHO, WHICH, THAT, WHOSE, WHOM

Exercise 1

She's the girl. She saw the accident.

| She's the girl | who | saw the accident. |
| | that | |

That's the car. It hit the bus.

| That's the car | which | hit the bus. |
| | that | |

1. She's the swimmer. She's just won the gold medal.
2. They're the keys. They open the locks on the door.
3. That's the travel agency. It gives extended credit.
4. Those are the astronauts. They were in orbit for six weeks.

Exercise 2

She's the girl. The police called her.
She's the girl the police called. or

| She's the girl | who | the police called. |
| | that | |

That's the car. She saw it.
That's the car she saw. or

| That's the car | which | she saw. |
| | that | |

1. These are the books. I use them in class.
2. They're the spies. The FBI has been watching them.
3. He's the criminal. The police are looking for him.
4. That's the name. I couldn't remember it yesterday.

Exercise 3

Ms. Lopez called Joe. She is the manager.
Ms. Lopez, who is the manager, called Joe.

The blue car hit the bus. It was a Ford.
The blue car, which was a Ford, hit the bus.

1. Those people saved my life. They pulled me from the burning car.
2. That woman travels everywhere by private jet. She's a multimillionaire.
3. That hotel's near the beach. It's the most expensive.
4. Those birds migrate to Antarctica. They breed near the North Pole.

Exercise 4

Joe got the job. Ms. Lopez called him.
Joe, who Ms. Lopez called, got the job.

The car hit the bus. He had only bought it the day before.

The car, which he had only bought the day before, hit the bus.

1. My parents send their regards. You met them last month.
2. The box contained a cake. They carried it carefully.
3. The game will be shown on TV tonight. It was taped this afternoon.
4. His sisters are identical twins. I saw them last year.

Exercise 5

The book is about Caroline Kennedy. Her father was President John Kennedy.
The book is about Caroline Kennedy whose father was President John Kennedy.

1. The movie is about two people. Their plane crashed in the jungle.
2. The play is about a woman. Her ambition was to conduct an orchestra.
3. The ballet was about a prince. His uncle hated him.
4. The song is about two young lovers. Their romance ended happily.

Exercise 6

My neighbor gave me some theater tickets. Her brother is an actor.
My neighbor, whose brother is an actor, gave me some theater tickets.

A woman from our town won the lottery. I teach her children.
A woman from our town, whose children I teach, won the lottery.

Look at this:

International Language Institute Napa Valley College, California		Course: English 202 Date: March 3				
Name	From	Native Language	Age	Arrival Date	Departure Date
Cruz, Teresa	Monterrey, Mexico	Spanish	21	1/15	6/15
Fereira, Paulo	Curitiba, Brazil	Portuguese	22	1/6	6/20
Fujikawa, Michiko	Osaka, Japan	Japanese	19	1/12	6/7
Nasser, Ibrahim	Muscat, Oman	Arabic	20	1/7	6/10

Exercise 8

1. *Teresa is the one who comes from Monterrey, Mexico.*
2. *She's the one who speaks Spanish.*
3. *She's the one who's leaving on June 15.*
4. *Teresa, who's from Monterrey, speaks Spanish.*
5. *Teresa, who speaks Spanish, is Mexican.*
6. *Teresa, who's Mexican, is 21.*

1. Charlie Chaplin died in 1977. His movies amused millions of people.
2. Ann Lee won the Oscar. I know her sister's ex-husband.
3. Our teacher speaks English perfectly. His parents are Chinese.
4. The Taylors have moved to Hawaii. We bought their house.

Exercise 7

She's the woman. I wrote to her.
She is the woman to whom I wrote. (Very formal)
She's the woman who/that I wrote to. (Less formal)
She's the woman I wrote to. (Familiar)

That's the hotel. I stayed in it.
That is the hotel in which I stayed.
That's the hotel which/that I stayed in.
That's the hotel I stayed in.

Transform these sentences, first in a formal style, then in a less formal one.

1. They are the people. I was talking about them.
2. That is the dog. I was afraid of it.
3. That is the mistake. I am complaining about it.
4. That is the tunnel. He went through it.
5. She is the police officer. The driver spoke to her.
6. There is the store. I bought my radio from it.
7. Ms. Lopez is the manager. I'm looking for her.

7. *Teresa, who's 21, arrived on January 15.*
8. *Teresa, who arrived on January 15, is leaving on June 15.*
9. *Teresa, whose native language is Spanish, is from Monterrey.*
10. *Monterrey, which is in Mexico, is Teresa's hometown.*

Make sentences about all the students.

Unit 50

DESCRIBING THINGS

Lost and Found

A: Union Station Lost and Found Department. Can I help you?

B: Oh, hello. Yes, I hope so. I left my briefcase on the train this morning. I wondered if it has been turned in.

A: Which train?

B: Oh, the 8:40 from Bradyville.

A: And what does your briefcase look like?

B: Well, it's—uh—an average-sized, rectangular, brown leather attaché case with brass locks.

A: We have quite a few that fit that description. Did it have your name on it?

B: No, not my name, but it has my initials by the handle: J. F. A.

A: Hold on just a minute. Let me take a look.

Exercise 1

Imagine you have lost something. Describe it to a partner without telling him/her what it is. Your partner has to guess.

Stolen Car

A: Police Department. Sergeant Wong speaking.

B: My car's been stolen! It's gone!

A: O.K. now, calm down. Let me have your name and address.

B: Richard Lockwood, 4512 Eisenhower Boulevard, Apartment 18J.

A: All right. Now, give me a description of the missing vehicle.

B: Well, it's an '84 Ford Escort—a light gray, four-door model. Oh, it has a thin dark blue stripe along the sides and a dent in the left front fender.

A: What's the license plate number?

B: RJG 1224

A: Hold on just a minute. . . . Hello? I have some good news and some bad news. The good news is that your car wasn't stolen. It was towed for illegal parking. The bad news is that it will cost you $80 to get it back.

Exercise 2

Describe somebody's car. Describe a car you would like to own.

The Real Estate Agent

A: Hello? Donna Woo speaking.

B: Hi, Donna. This is Joyce Fein at Ivy Realty. I think I've found a house you'll be interested in.

A: Oh, terrific! What's it like? Tell me about it.

B: Well, it's in Arrowhead, the section you wanted. It's a split-level, three-bedroom, red-brick house with white trim. It's only six years old and has a large country-style kitchen.

A: How big a yard does it have?

B: It's a one-acre lot with some nice-sized trees and a very pretty flower garden in back. When do you want to see it?

A: It sounds good. Could we meet there tomorrow afternoon?

B: Sure thing. Let's make it at 2 o'clock.

Exercise 3

Describe somebody's house. Describe a house you would like to live in.

Exercise 4

Describe these living rooms. Describe your ideal living room/kitchen/bedroom/bathroom. Describe the furniture you would put in it and where you would put it. Describe a restaurant that you've been to. Describe your classroom.

Exercise 5

Describe an object to a partner using the diagram below. Your partner has to guess what it is.

Note: This diagram shows the usual order of adjectives. You won't often find them all in one sentence.

How much/many?	What's it like?	How big is it?	What shape is it?	How old is it?	What color is it?		What's the pattern on it?	Where's it from?	What's it made of?	What is it?
a/an	beautiful	little	square	old	pale	red	check	French	plastic	scarf
one	nice	small	round	new	light	yellow	striped	English	cotton	shirt
three	ugly	medium-sized	oval	modern	bright	green	plain	Japanese	wood(en)	chair
some	clean	average-sized	rectangular	antique	dark	blue	flowered	Mexican	leather	car
a few	dirty	large	pointed	19th century		pink	polka-dot	Italian	gold	house
several	cheap	big	triangular	1930s		black		American	metal	box
a lot of	expensive	long	flat	1982		white		Chinese	paper	

DESCRIBING PEOPLE

Listen to these people talking about their friends. Look at the example. Complete the other columns.

Name	Donna	Chuck	Janet	Bob
Age	late teens			
Build	good figure			
Height	pretty tall			
Hair color	black			
Hairstyle	long, wavy			
Face	oval-shaped, turned-up nose, full lips			
Eyes	blue, long eyelashes			
Complexion	olive-skinned			
Distinguishing features	dimples			
Dress				
Personality	talkative, funny			

Look at this:

Age	Build	Height	Hair Color	Hairstyle	Face	Distinguishing features	Personality
young	fat	5'7" ("5 foot 7")	black	long	thin	beard (M)	nice
middle-aged	thin	medium height	brown	short	long	mustache (M)	quiet
elderly	slim	average height	red	straight	round	sideburns (M)	loud
old	plump	tall	blonde	wavy	oval	unshaven (M)	reserved
in his/her 30's	medium-build	short	gray	curly	square	clean-shaven (M)	calm
in his/her late teens	well-built		white	parted on the left	high cheekbones	a scar	moody
in his/her mid-20's	broad-shouldered		dyed	neat	high forehead	a beauty-mark	(un)sociable
in his/her early 40's	overweight		a blonde	windblown	thin lips	a mole	sophisticated
	big-boned		a redhead	with braids	full lips	with freckles	funny
	petite		redheaded	with bangs	long nose	with dimples	cheerful
	skinny		dark	swept back	straight nose	with wrinkles	polite
			light	in a bun (F)	turned-up nose	with lines	reliable
				pony-tail	broken nose	with glasses	talkative
				bald (M)	flat nose	well made-up (F)	confident
				balding (M)	a cleft chin	heavily made-up (F)	aggressive
				thinning	a pointed chin		friendly
				receding (M)	double chin		shy

Eyes	Complexion	Dress
blue	pale	scruffy
gray	suntanned	well-dressed
brown	olive-skinned	casual
long eyelashes	light-skinned	conservative
thick eyelashes/brows	Oriental	elegant
bushy eyebrows/lashes	dark-skinned	fashionable
thin eyebrows/lashes	black	

Describe these people. Describe yourself, another student, a famous person.

THE STATE OF THE UNION

The President of the United States is required by law to deliver a State of the Union message once a year. This takes place in the middle of January before a joint session of Congress. The President discusses the condition of the country and outlines his plans for the coming year. The areas he touches on are the economy, government expenditures, science and technology, environmental protection, education, crime prevention, welfare, and foreign relations. The purpose of the address is to ask members of the Senate and the House of Representatives as well as the American people for their support in the coming year.

A Few Hours before the President's Speech

Julie: Hi, Gary. How come you're late?

Gary: The battery was dead. Al from the garage came with jumper cables. Then I went back to the garage to get some gas—and to get the battery recharged.

Julie: Oh, no! Do we need a new one?

Gary: Probably.

Julie: Not another expense! If it's not one thing, it's another!

Gary: Well, let's watch TV to see the President's State of the Union address.

Julie: Not me. Last year I watched it in order to get some good news. Not this year! You're on your own.

Exercise 1
garage
He went to the garage to get some gas.

Make sentences with:
1. bank
2. drugstore
3. library
4. newsstand
5. bakery
6. vegetable stand
7. post office
8. supermarket
9. butcher's
10. florist's

The Morning after the Speech

Julie: Steve, come here, please.

Steve: What is it, Mom?

Julie: I'm sending you to the store to get a few things. O.K.?

Steve: Sure. Should I go to Shopway or Foodcity?

Julie: Foodcity. The prices are lower, and after the President's speech last night, I think we'll shop at Foodcity in order to save some money. We have to cut down on expenses.

Steve: I thought you didn't want to watch the President last night.

Julie: I didn't. I read the speech in the paper this morning. I read it to feel better. Now I feel worse.

Exercise 2
He/her/post office/stamps.
He sent her to the post office to get some stamps.
Continue
1. They/him/newsstand/magazine.
2. She/them/bank/quarters.
3. My boss/me/stationery store/paper.
4. We/Pete/supermarket/fruit.

The Evening after the Speech

Gary: Steve, turn on the TV, please. I want to hear the news report on the President's speech.

Steve: O.K., Dad.

News reporter: In his State of the Union message the President outlined his plans for the year. He proposes to decrease domestic spending in order to reduce deficits. He wants to simplify the tax code for the purpose of treating all taxpayers more fairly. To encourage a great leap forward in scientific research in space, he wants to develop a permanent space station. He demands an increase in the environmental protection budget in order to reduce pollution. His main interest is children, and he wants to establish a bipartisan commission on education in order to improve the schools.

Exercise 3
In order to reduce deficits, he will decrease domestic spending.
For the purpose of reducing deficits, he will decrease domestic spending.
He will decrease domestic spending in order to reduce deficits.
He will decrease domestic spending for the purpose of reducing deficits.
Make sentences in each of these four ways about each proposal in the table below.

Proposal	Purpose
Decrease domestic spending	Reduce deficits
Simplify tax code	Treat all taxpayers more fairly
Develop permanent space station	Encourage scientific research
Increase environmental protection budget	Develop new techniques to reduce pollution
Establish a bipartisan commission on education	Improve schools
Enforce tougher punishments for criminals	Encourage a decline in the crime rate
Reduce nuclear arms	Promote international peace
Provide tuition tax credits	Expand opportunities for low income families
Intensify drive against child abuse	Protect youngsters
Create more child care centers	Aid working mothers

DO-IT-YOURSELF

Do-It-Yourself magazine sponsors a contest every summer to find the winner of the annual "Do-It-Yourself" Award. This year a married couple won. They are Rudy and Irene Cipriani. A writer and a photographer have come to their house. The writer is interviewing the Ciprianis for an article in the magazine.

Writer: Well, I'm very impressed by all the work you've done on your house. How long have you been working on it?

Rudy: We first became interested in do-it-yourself several years ago. You see, our son Paul is a paraplegic. He's in a wheelchair, and so we just had to make changes in the house. There was no way we could afford to pay to have it done. We had to learn to do it ourselves.

Writer: Did you have any experience with this kind of work? Did you have any practical skills?

Rudy: No. We got a few books from the library, but they didn't help much. Then I decided to go to a vocational school at night so that I could learn cabinetmaking and electrical wiring. Later Irene went so that she could study plumbing and general carpentry too.

Writer: So tell me about the kind of changes you made to the house.

Irene: First of all, practical things to help Paul. You never realize the problems handicapped people have until it affects your own family. Nowadays most public buildings have ramps so that people in wheelchairs can get in, and buses have lifts so that handicapped people can get on and off. But just imagine the problems Paul would have in your house. We needed wide halls so that he could move from one room to another. And we needed a big bathroom so that he could be as independent as possible. We had to change so much.

Writer: Where did you start?

Irene: The electrical system. Rudy completely rewired the house so that Paul could turn on and off the lights and plug in appliances. We had to lower the switches and raise the outlets. We had to redo the whole house so that Paul could reach things and do what he wanted.

Writer: What else did you do?

Rudy: By the time we had made all the changes for Paul, do-it-yourself had become our hobby. We enjoyed doing things around the house and doing them together. Even Paul got into it. He's learned a lot about fixing things and keeping our tools in good shape. He came up with an idea to connect the smoke alarm to a separate light system. When the smoke alarm goes off, a light goes on in every hallway. We did that so that we could see the way out of the house if there was a fire. He also has a remote control device on his wheelchair so that he can open and close the front and back doors.

Writer: What are you working on now?

Irene: We've just finished redoing the kitchen so that Paul can do a little cooking. Now we're converting the garage into a workshop so that he can make some money fixing appliances.

Writer: There's a $50,000 prize that goes with your title. How do you plan to spend the money?

Irene: We're hoping to start our own building business so that we can do conversions for the handicapped. We think we've become experts.

Look at this:

| I did this so that | he
she | could
couldn't | do that. |
| | this
that | would
wouldn't | happen. |

| I'm doing this
I do this | so that | he
she | can
can't | do that. |
| | | this
that | will
won't | happen. |

or

| So that | he
she | could
couldn't | do that, | I did
this. |
| | this
that | would
wouldn't | happen, | |

| So that | he
she | can
can't | do that, | I'm doing
this. |
| | this
that | will
won't | happen, | I do this. |

Exercise 1
These are some of the things the Ciprianis did. Look at the chart, ask questions with *Why?/ What's the purpose of . . . ?* and answer them.

Improvement	Purpose
put in swinging doors	Paul could push through with his wheelchair.
widen doors	The wheelchair could get through.
install phones in every room	Paul could always get to one.
enlarge bathroom	Paul could use it.
lower light switches	Paul could reach them.
put in ramps	The wheelchair could get in and out.
design remote control device	Paul could open and close the front door.

Exercise 2
Here are some of the things the Ciprianis are going to do. Ask questions and answer them.

Plan	Purpose
install an elevator	He'll be able to get upstairs on his own.
convert garage into workshop	He'll be able to make some money.
install lift on van	The wheelchair will be able to get in and out.
design a beeper system	He can call us any time.
build a toolshed in backyard	We'll have somewhere to keep everything.

BE CAREFUL!

Look at this:

Do this	so that you don't	do that.
	in order not to	

Do this	to	avoid	that.
	in order to		doing that.
	so that you can		

Do this	to prevent	that (from happening).
	to stop	something (from)
	to keep	happening.
		somebody (from) doing
		that.

Exercise 1

Look at the expressions in Mandangan. Practice with a partner using:

How do you say (this) in Mandangan?
Can you translate (this) into Mandangan?
What does (that) mean in English?

Exercise 2

Why should we keep plastic bags away from babies?
To avoid the danger of suffocation.
or
To prevent babies from suffocating themselves.
Look at the table above. Ask questions about these warning labels, and answer them.

CONSTRUCTION TECHNOLOGIES INTERNATIONAL INC.
Biloxi, Mississippi
Danga River Irrigation Project
Republic of Mandanga

Advice to employees going to Mandanga for the first time.

MEDICAL PRECAUTIONS

1. To avoid the possibility of infection, have your doctor give you shots for typhoid, cholera, and yellow fever before departure.
2. Mandanga is a malarial area. To prevent malaria, start taking Aralen tablets two weeks before departure. Take one every week while in Mandanga — always on the same day of the week at the same time.
3. When in camp, always use a net to keep mosquitoes from biting you while you are sleeping.
4. Also to prevent mosquito and other insect bites, use insect repellent on exposed parts of your body.
5. Mandanga is a tropical country and certain precautions should be taken at work:
   (a) To prevent heat exhaustion, be sure to drink adequate quantities of liquids.
   (b) Take salt tablets to avoid getting dehydrated.
   (c) Limit the time you spend working in direct sunlight in order to prevent sunstroke.
6. To avoid infection, water should be boiled or purified with iodine tablets.
7. In order not to be infected by parasites, eat only cooked vegetables and peeled fruits.

LOCAL CUSTOMS

1. Avoid wearing shorts or bathing suits in religious buildings.
2. Remove your shoes before entering private homes to avoid offending the householder.
3. Never hang clothes out to dry in public so that you don't offend people passing by.
4. You should avoid wearing bikinis, or other very brief bathing suits.
5. In order not to appear rude, learn a few expressions in Mandangan before your arrival there.
   Here are a few essential expressions:

Yo bro.	Hello.
Lay tah.	Goodbye.
Yep.	Yes.
Nope.	No.
Ka mon.	Please.
Kul man.	Thank you.
Oop zee.	Excuse me.
Lu kin gud.	It's nice to see you.
Hiya du in?	How are you?
Oh key doe key.	Very well.

WARNING:
This is **NOT** a toy.

To avoid danger of suffocation keep this plastic bag away from babies and young children.

Supertrack stereo stylus

ST 800E

Check your stylus regularly to avoid damaging your valuable records. Change it at the first sign of wear.

TEFL
Non-stick frying pan
To avoid scratching this pan, always use wooden or plastic utensils. Avoid using metal utensils at all times.

NATIONAL EXPRESS
Here is your new National Express Credit Card. To prevent unauthorized use by others, sign it immediately and take care of it as if it were money. To avoid fraudulent use of your old card, cut it in half and dispose of it! Never leave home without it!

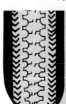

Goodstone Tires
To prevent undue wear and tear always check the air pressure of your tires. At regular intervals rotate your tires to avoid uneven wear.

GLASEX CASSEROLE DISH WARNING
To prevent breakage, after baking let dish sit at room temperature for 20 minutes before refrigerating.

TEXOIL
Motor Oil
To prevent undue engine wear, always change oil at regular intervals.

ZENO Cassette Player

WARNING: To prevent fire or shock hazard, do not expose this appliance to rain or moisture.

Announcer: Tonight on "TV Close-Up" we'll be talking to some rat race dropouts. Our correspondent Vicky Romero talks to some very happy people who dropped out of the rat race to start a new way of life.

Vicky: I'm here in Northern Vermont, where the nearest town is 25 miles away, and it's only a post office, a general store, a few houses, a school and a church. It's not easy to farm this rocky land, but Dan and Michelle Gallagher are doing just that. Dan and Michelle were born and lived most of their lives in New York City. Dan was vice-president of marketing for a publishing company, and Michelle was an advertising executive. They gave up their jobs and moved to this remote area of Vermont four years ago. Michelle, what made you give everything up for this?

Michelle: Everything? That's a matter of opinion. An apartment on Park Avenue and a beach house on Long Island isn't everything. We used to work long hours. We came home so late at night that we hardly ever saw each other. We should have done this years ago, but we were making so much money that we were afraid to quit our jobs. Even the time we spent at the beach house was so hectic that we never had time to just be together. Go, go, go all the time. So four years ago we got in the car and decided to go where nobody we knew would be. We ended up here in Vermont and saw this place. It was for sale, and we liked it so much we decided to buy it. The next week we quit our jobs, sold most of our things, and here we are!

Vicky: How do you earn a living?

Michelle: We don't need a lot. We have two milk cows and a few chickens. We grow all our own vegetables. It's a simple life, and we're not trying to make a profit. We're still so busy that we work from daylight to dark, but we're together. And now we have Kimberly, who's three. We're happier than we've ever been.

Vicky: There must be some things you miss.

Michelle: Not really. We knew a lot of people in New York, but most of them weren't really friends. We see our neighbors now and then, and we're having such a good time here that we never feel lonely. Oh, sometimes I think about the theater or

A NEW WAY OF LIFE

the ballet, but between Kimberly and PBS I have more than enough entertainment.

Vicky: The motocycle I'm sitting on is a very special one. Special because it's been all the way around the world. It belongs to Luke Sztanko who has just come back here to Detroit after a three-year motorcycle trip. Luke, what led you to quit your job and make this trip?

Luke: I worked in a car factory on the assembly line. It was really monotonous. It was such a routine that I never had to think. My job is done by a robot now. Little wonder. Anyway, I bought this bike secondhand, put two packs on the back, and got myself on a freighter to Europe.

Vicky: What did you do for money?

Luke: I had a little money saved up, but of course it didn't last long. I had to find work where I could. I did many different things—picked fruit, washed dishes, worked as a mechanic, played the guitar—I even taught English.

Vicky: How did people react to you—in India, for example?

Luke: Everywhere I went, the people were so friendly that problems seemed to solve themselves. There was such a tremendous amount of interest in the bike that it was easy to start a conversation. Usually, you can communicate without knowing

the language.

Vicky: Did you ever feel like giving up and coming home?

Luke: Only once, in Bangladesh. I got so sick from something I ate that I had to go to a hospital. But it didn't last long.

Vicky: You've had such an exciting time that you'll find it hard to settle down in Detroit, won't you?

Luke: I'm not going to. Next week I'm leaving again, but this time I'm heading south—to Tierra del Fuego. See you when I get back!

Exercise 1
The people were very friendly. He felt welcome.
The people were so friendly that he felt welcome.
Continue.
1. He was very old. He couldn't walk.
2. She was very busy. She didn't stop for lunch.
3. She was very late. She missed the plane.
4. He was very sick. He couldn't go out.
5. She had spent too much money. She couldn't afford another trip.
6. There were too many people in the boat. It sank.

Exercise 2
The farm was so beautiful that they bought it.
It was such a beautiful farm that they bought it.
Continue.
1. The book was so interesting that she couldn't stop reading it.
2. The problems were so hard that nobody could solve them.
3. The doctor was so friendly that everybody liked her.
4. The dog was so mean that the letter carrier wouldn't deliver the mail.
5. The box was so heavy that he couldn't lift it.
6. The trip was so exciting that he's going again.

Exercise 3
She was such a good tennis player that nobody ever beat her.
The tennis player was so good that nobody ever beat her.
Continue.
1. It was such a dangerous job that nobody would do it.
2. He was such a good dancer that he won the prize.
3. They were such boring programs that nobody watched them.
4. It was such a crazy story that nobody believed it.

Unit 56

LAST OF THE AIRSHIPS?

At 7:20 p.m. on May 6, 1937, the world's largest airship, the *Hindenburg*, floated majestically over Lakehurst Airport, New Jersey, after an uneventful crossing from Frankfurt, Germany. There were 97 people on board for the first Atlantic crossing of the season. There were a number of reporters waiting to greet it. Suddenly radio listeners heard the commentator screaming, "Oh, my God! It's broken into flames. It's flashing ... flashing. It's flashing terribly." 32 seconds later the airship had disintegrated and 35 people were dead. The Age of the Airship was over.

The *Hindenburg* was the last in a series of airships which had been developed over 40 years in both Europe and the United States. They were designed to carry passengers and cargo over long distances. The *Hindenburg* could carry 50 passengers accommodated in 25 luxury cabins with all the amenities of a first class hotel. All the cabins had hot and cold water and electric heating. There was a dining room, a bar, and a lounge with a dance floor and a baby grand piano. The *Hindenburg* had been built to compete with the great luxury transatlantic liners. It was 804 feet (245 m) long with a diameter of 135 feet (41 m). It could cruise at a speed of 78 mph (125 km/h), and was able to cross the Atlantic in less than half the time of a liner. By

1937 it had carried 1000 passengers safely and had even transported circus animals and cars. Its sister ship, the *Graf Zeppelin*, had flown over a million miles (1.5 million km), and it had carried 13,100 passengers without incident.

The *Hindenburg* was filled with hydrogen, which is a highly flammable gas, and every safety precaution had been taken to prevent accidents. It had a smoking room which was pressurized in order to prevent gas from ever entering it. The cigarette lighters were chained to the tables, and both passengers and crew were searched for matches before entering the ship. Special materials, which were used in the construction of the airship, had been chosen to minimize the possibility of accidental sparks, which might cause an explosion.

Nobody knows the exact cause of the *Hindenburg* disaster. Sabotage has been suggested, but experts at the time believed that it was caused by leaking gas which was ignited by static electricity. It had been waiting to land for three hours because of heavy thunderstorms. The explosion happened just as the first mooring rope, which was wet, touched the ground. Observers saw the first flames appear near the tail, and the fire began to spread quickly along the hull. There were a

number of flashes as the hydrogen-filled compartments exploded. The airship sank to the ground. The most surprising thing is that 62 people managed to escape. The fatalities were highest among the crew members, many of whom were working deep inside the airship. After the *Hindenburg* disaster, all airships were grounded, and until recently, they have never been seriously considered as a commercial proposition.

Airships—Achievements and Disasters

1852 1st airship (144 ft. long) flew over Paris.

1910 —14 Five Zeppelin airships operated commercial flights within Germany, carrying 35,000 people without injury.

1914 —18 Military Zeppelins took part in 53 bombing raids on London, during First World War.

1919 British "R34." First transatlantic crossing. Both directions (6,330 mi. in 183 hours).

1925 U.S. *Shenandoah* (first helium airship) destroyed in a storm over Ohio. Heavy loss of life.

1926 Italian airship, the *Norge,* flew over North Pole.

1929 German *Graf Zeppelin* flew around the world. Began commercial transatlantic flights.

1930 British "R101" (775 ft. long) crashed in France. Killed 48 out of 54 on board. British airship program cancelled.

1931 U.S. *Akron* in service in USA —could carry 207 passengers.

1933 *Akron* wrecked in a storm.

1935 Sister ship, U.S. *Macon* wrecked.

1936 *Hindenburg* built. Carried 117 passengers in one flight.

1937 *Hindenburg* crashed.

1938 *Graf Zeppelin II* completed. It never entered service.

1940 Both *Graf Zeppelins* scrapped.

1958 U.S. Navy built a radar airship, the "ZPG-3W." (404 ft. long, 21 crew).

1960 "ZPG-3W" crashed in the ocean.

1961 U.S. Navy airship program ended.

Present Goodyear operates the only airships (called "blimps") in the world: the *America,* the *Enterprise,* the *Columbia* and the *Europa.*

EATING OUT

Eating Out
Mimi Hilton

The Blue Mill
133 West River St., 730-8375
All major credit cards.
Closed Monday.
Reservations recommended.

This three-month-old restaurant has attracted attention because it is a restored, one hundred fifty-year-old mill. The decor is charming and warm in an Early American, country style. Although the tables and chairs are modern reproductions, there are enough authentic antique pieces at the entrance and on the walls to avoid the fake Disneyland look of some restorations.

The menu is also very American, though it is a bit too traditional for my taste. The menu also is very extensive, which always worries me because a large menu often means a large freezer. Although my dinner companions and I chose some things from the regular menu, we usually chose one of the day's specials.

The most delicious main course we tried was the country stew which consisted of potatoes, carrots, peas, mushrooms, very tender beef, and — surprise! — some smoked pork sausage. Because top quality beef was used, it was unusually good. Among other well-prepared main courses was the fried chicken because it wasn't cooked before and then re-heated. It was fresh and crisp.

The vegetables that came with the main courses were fresh but overcooked. The only exception was the string beans which were green and crisp (a mistake?).

Because the main courses are so large, there is really no need for an appetizer or soup. But for big eaters, I can recommend the mixed salad. The clam chowder was tasty because it was homemade, but it had no special distinction. The oysters on the half-shell were nicely served on a bed of ice, although I would prefer to have a better sauce for them.

If you can still eat dessert after all this plus rather good homemade bread and creamery butter, try the apple pie. The apples were juicy and firm and the pastry was light.

It's hard to judge the service at this friendly restaurant. Because it was so crowded when I went, usually at 8 o'clock, service was slow. The reservation system doesn't always work. On one occasion, someone took our reservation for dinner but didn't have it when we arrived. This kind of thing can damage a restaurant's reputation, although its food may be good.

Diner's Journal
by Roger Mitchell

NEW FAST FOOD CHAIN ARRIVES

The Nashville Superburger chain, which started in the Tennessee city six years ago, opened its first store here last weekend on Commerce Street between Grant and Taylor Streets. I was interested to see the connection between Nashville, the capital of country music, and hamburgers. Would the burgers be Southern fried? Would they be served on biscuits or with grits? Would they be shaped like guitars? Well, I've been there twice and didn't find any real difference between Nashville Superburgers and McDonald's, Burger King, or Wendy's.

The place was so brightly lit that I wished I had brought my sunglasses. Once I got used to the light, I liked the green and orange decor, usually found in health food places. Because those colors mean yogurt and alfalfa sprouts, I felt good and almost healthy about having fast food. Plus, the place was spotlessly clean — almost antiseptic.

Although there were long lines, service was incredibly fast. The menu is limited to a variety of hamburgers, and the prices are reasonable. I had the "Super-Duper-Burger," which was served with lettuce and tomato. Although the meat itself was rather gray and tasteless, the "secret relish" made it passable. The french fries were the best I've ever eaten at a fast food restaurant.

Everybody seemed to be drinking milkshakes, and although I usually shy away from them in fast food places I felt I should try one. It was thick and sweet — and there was probably not one drop of natural milk in it. Even though these may be low in cholesterol, I want whole milk, real ice cream, and natural flavorings in my milkshakes. Although I am as concerned as anyone else about health, I'll fight the cholesterol battle somewhere else.

Nashville Superburger is a sure bet when you're downtown and in a hurry. I was in and out in ten minutes. It reminded me of a highway filling station.

TODAY'S BLUE MILL SPECIALS

SOUP: NEW ORLEANS GUMBO $2.50

APPETIZER: OYSTERS ON THE HALF SHELL $4.50

ENTREES:
GARDEN STEW $8.95
SIRLOIN STEAK $10.95

Nashville Superburger Bar

1. Nashville Burger (2 oz.)		$1.29
2. Nashville Big Burger (4 oz.)		$1.49
3. Nashville Super Burger (6 oz.)		$1.89
4. Nashville Super-Duper Burger (10 oz.)		$2.10
5. Nashville Cheeseburger		$1.39
6. Nashville Super Cheeseburger		$1.99
7. Nashville Super-Duper Cheeseburger		$2.20

All served with Nashville Secret Relish

French Fries				
Regular		$.75		
Large		.89		
Beverages				
Milkshakes	vanilla		$.89	
	chocolate		.89	
	strawberry		.89	
		Small	Medium	Large
Pepsi-Cola		$.50	$.65	$.75
Seven-up		.50	.65	.75
Coffee		.50		.75

Have a Nice Day!

Look at this:

It was raining. She took her umbrella.
She took her umbrella because it was raining.

It wasn't raining. He took his umbrella.

He took his umbrella	although though even though	it wasn't raining.

Exercise

Now combine these sentences with "because" or "although."

1. He didn't take the job. The salary was good.
2. Mark wasn't thirsty. He drank some milk.
3. They're afraid of flying. They flew to New York.
4. Sarah needed a new calculator. She bought one.

Unit 58

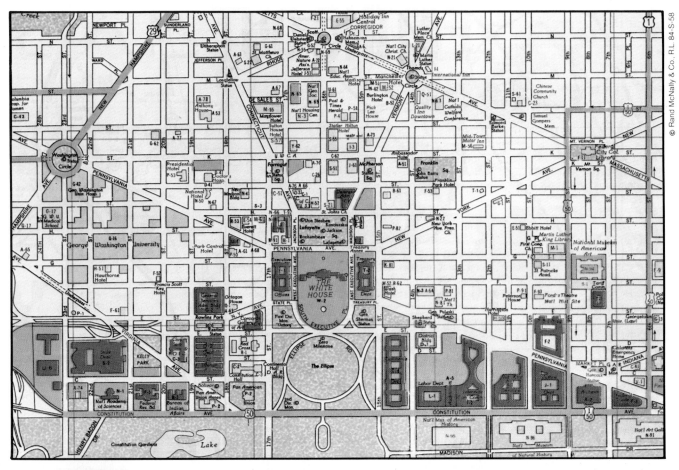

FINDING YOUR WAY AROUND

D.C. Hackers

Becoming a Washington, D.C. cab driver or "hacker" isn't easy. In order to get a license to drive a taxi in Washington, candidates have to pass a detailed examination. They have to learn not only the streets, landmarks, and hotels, but also the best way to get to them. They are examined not only on the routes, but also on the best routes at different times of day. D.C. cabs or "hacks" don't have meters. Passengers are charged according to how many zones they are driven through. So candidates have to learn all the zones and the rates. People who want to pass the examinations spend much of their free time driving around Washington, studying maps, and learning the huge street directory by heart.

Marcus Johnson and Gail Graham are going to take the exam next week. They're asking each other questions that could be on the exam. Listen to Gail's question and try to follow Marcus's directions on the map.

Gail: O.K., Marcus. Ready? You're outside the White House on Pennsylvania Avenue, and you've just picked up a passenger who wants to go to the International Inn at Thomas Circle. Use the most direct route.

Marcus: I'd go east on Pennsylvania Avenue and turn left on 15th Street. I'd continue on to Thomas Circle. The International Inn is half way around Thomas Circle.

Exercise 1

Now practice with a partner. Point out your departure point on the map, state your destination and ask your partner to direct you.

Unit 59

The Metro

Traveling on the Washington Metro presents few difficulties for visitors because of the clear color-coded map. At the bottom of the map you will find fare and travel time information. You buy your farecard at one of the yellow vending machines. You can use nickels, dimes, quarters, one-dollar and five-dollar bills, and the machine will give you change. You have to use your farecard to enter the Metro system by inserting it into the slot at the gate. It will be returned to you at the other side of the gate. Do the same thing when exiting the system.

Listen to these people talking about the Metro map, and follow their routes on the map.

Piero and Margherita have just arrived at National Airport.

Piero: O.K. We have to get to Deanwood. Can you see it?

Margherita: Yes, it's up here. It looks so easy. We just take the Yellow Line to L'Enfant Plaza, then change to the Orange Line. It goes straight there. It's the seventh stop from L'Enfant Plaza.

Betsy is at the information booth at the Pentagon.

Betsy: Excuse me. How do I get to Connecticut Avenue and Q Street? I mean, which is the nearest Metro station?

Attendant: You want Dupont Circle. Take a look at the map. You take the Yellow Line to Gallery Place. Then you'll have to change for the Red Line. It's the third stop.

Betsy: I see.

Attendant: Or you could take the Blue Line to Metro Center and change to the Red Line there.

Betsy: Which way is faster?

Attendant: It's about the same.

Betsy: Well, thank you.

Alice and Fred are at Capital Heights.

Fred: Where's a map?

Alice: There's one over here. They said we have to meet them at Farragut North. Can you find it?

Fred: Yes, here it is. I guess we take the Blue Line to L'Enfant Plaza, then change to the Yellow Line and go to Gallery Place. Then we go two stops to Farragut North.

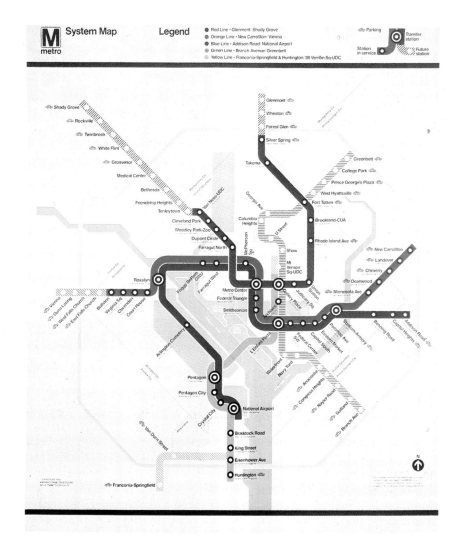

Alice: I'm not sure that's the quickest way. We could take the Blue Line all the way to Metro Center and get the Red Line there. Then it's only one stop.

Fred: We might as well do it your way. It's only eleven stops. My way has twelve stops.

Exercise 2

Practice with a partner. Give directions from:

1. Courthouse to National Airport
2. Federal Triangle to Union Station
3. Potomac Avenue to Gallery Place
4. Dupont Circle to Rosslyn
5. Union Station to Arlington Cemetary
6. Brookland to Courthouse

Exercise 3

Here are some famous Washington, D.C. landmarks with their nearest Metro stations. Make conversations about getting to them from: (a) Deanwood, (b) National Airport, and (c) Union Station.

1. The FBI—Federal Bureau of Investigation (Metro Center)
2. The Kennedy Center (Foggy Bottom—GWU)
3. The Washington Monument (Smithsonian)
4. The RFK Stadium (Stadium Armory)
5. The National Air and Space Museum (L'Enfant Plaza)
6. The Freer Gallery (Smithsonian)

Exercise 4

Practice with a partner. State a departure point and destination. Your partner has to give you directions.

Channel 7 in Portstown presents the Six O'Clock Report with anchor, Jack Dennehy.

Good evening. Thousands of Portstown residents marched on City Hall today to protest plans to build a state prison near the city. Although a light rain was falling, an estimated five thousand people marched over a mile from the Portstown High School to City Hall, where Governor Brown and Mayor Henry Flores were meeting to discuss the project. A new prison is needed because the two other state prisons are overcrowded. Several sites for the new prison were considered, but Portstown was chosen because, in the Governor's words, "All areas in the state must share the problems of our prison system." Although the protestors asked to meet with the Governor, he refused and returned to the capital. After the Governor's departure, however, the Mayor met with the organizers of the march and explained his position. An unidentified aide to the Governor said that another site will probably be chosen in the end.

Four entire city blocks were evacuated this afternoon in the Oceanside section because of a gas explosion. The explosion occurred at 1:20 p.m. in a deserted building on 2nd Street. Fire Department officials believe that the explosion was due to leaking gas. The building had been empty for several months, and they suspect that a gas main had cracked because of vibrations from work being carried out by the city on the street. Windows 300 feet away were broken by the blast. The police have blocked off the area until the Fire Department and Portstown Gas Company complete their investigation.

Coast Guard helicopters went into action today after a yacht capsized in Coolidge Sound. Despite rain and high seas, the helicopters were able to rescue all but one of those aboard. Two men and two women were pulled to safety, but one of the men was dead on arrival despite the rescue team's efforts. The other three are in satisfactory condition. The fifth passenger, a woman, was not found. Although the Coast Guard continue their search, she is presumed drowned. All names are withheld pending notification of families. The Coast Guard had issued a small craft warning this morning, but the yacht set out from the Newgate Marina despite the warnings.

THE SIX O'CLOCK NEWS

Central Motors announced today that they are shutting down their plant in Plattsburg. Fourteen hundred workers will be laid off because of the closing down of the plant, which is due to a sharp decline in sales of Central Motors' J car. In spite of union's acceptance of minimal salary increases last year, the shutdown became inevitable because of the cancellation of most orders for the J car. Due to competition from cheaper foreign-made cars, J car dealers have not been able to sell the cars they have in stock. Plattsburg Mayor Bob Goodall predicted that hundreds of other jobs will be affected as suppliers and merchants feel the effects of the lost payroll.

Incomplete reports have reached this station about a 100-mph car chase on Portstown streets and roads north of here. Only minutes ago, according to these reports, Portstown police were alerted by an anonymous phone call and rushed to catch a gang that was breaking into a local discount clothing store. However, the gang of young white males escaped in a late-model car that allegedly had been stolen two days ago in Harbor City. The gang was armed and fired several times at the police cars behind them. Never-

theless, the police were able to run the gang's car off the road and arrest all the members with no injuries on either side. We have no more details at this time.

Turning now to sports: The Portstown High School stadium was filled last night when the Portstown Pirates played their traditional rivals, the Harbor City Raiders. Pirate quarterback Tony Rizzuto scored two touchdowns in the first half. Although the Raiders didn't score at all in the first half, they went on to win with two touchdowns and a field goal in the second half. Raider halfback Billy Carlysle was limping at the end of the first half because of a fall, but nevertheless ran a total of 87 yards in the second half and scored one of the two Raider touchdowns. As the game entered the last minutes of play, the referees penalized both teams because of unnecessary roughness. In spite of the Pirates' good showing in the first half, they couldn't seem to do anything right in the second. The final score: Pirates 14, Raiders 17.

Look at this:

It was snowing, so they canceled the game.
or

He canceled the game	because it was snowing.	
	because of	the snow.
	due to	

or

Because it was snowing,	he canceled the game.	
Because of	the snow,	
Due to		

It was snowing, but they didn't cancel the game.
or

He didn't cancel the game	although it was snowing.	
	in spite of	the snow.
	despite	

or

Although it was snowing,	he didn't cancel the game.	
In spite of	the snow,	
Despite		

It was hard, but she managed to win.
or

It was hard.	However,	she managed to win.
	Nevertheless,	

or

It was hard. She managed to win	however.
	nevertheless.

or

It was hard. She managed,	however,	to win.
	nevertheless,	

Exercise
Now write today's news for your local area.

ALL THE GOOD NEWS

THE BRIDGEPORT TIMES, THURSDAY, JANUARY 1

Our New Year's News Present to the President

The President, speaking at the American Bar Association Convention this year, asked why newspapers only print the bad news. "Why don't they tell us things like how many planes landed safely in the U.S. in one day?" he asked. Here is our New Year's present to the President — a column of good news items.

★ In 1921 Alice Hoover Meyers, now 88 years old, began writing her first novel about life in a small Kansas town. Last week Milburn University Press published the 1,500 page novel, *The Women in the Club*, more than 60 years after Mrs. Meyers put pen to paper. When asked about her reaction to becoming a published author at age 88, Mrs. Meyers replied, "I hope there's time to write the next one!"

★ O'Hare Airport in Chicago, the busiest airport in the United States, reports that a total of 645,586 planes took off and landed without incident during the year.

★ Eleven Korean children with congenital heart defects, flown to the U.S. under the auspices of the American Medical Association, were successfully operated on last week at Houston General Hospital in Texas. After a brief convalescence, they will be flown back to Seoul. The A.M.A., which is sponsoring the "Big Heart" program, plans to help many other children from all over the world.

★ Sally K. Ride became the first American woman astronaut in space as a member of the Challenger Space Shuttle crew on a flight that lasted six days.

★ The Governor of California announced last week at a meeting of 200 state legislators that the state treasury has a surplus of over $200 million with nearly $1 billion projected for next year. This is an amazing accomplishment in view of the condition of the state treasury six months ago — a $1.5 million deficit! The Governor has won the support of voters all over the state.

★ After a lapse of 117 years, the United States has established full diplomatic relations with the Vatican.

★ According to reports, there were 2,439,000 civil and religious marriage ceremonies this year, an increase of 1% over the total for last year.

★ A total of 460,348 immigrants from all over the world were admitted to the United States this year.

★ Sandra Day O'Connor, the first female United States Supreme Court Justice, has won a poll conducted by the *World Almanac*. She has been voted the most influential woman in the United States.

★ In January as usual, the President delivered his State of the Union message to the House of Representatives and the Senate in a joint session of Congress. This year was special, however, because it marked the beginning of the 100th Congress.

★ The Chinese premier visited the United States this year, the highest-ranking Peking official ever to visit this country. In a welcoming ceremony at the White House the Premier said, "I come as a friendly envoy of the Chinese people for the purpose of seeking mutual understanding."

★ Even farmers are smiling — that is, the soybean farmers who were able to bring in a record harvest last year with a minimum effort — over 2¼ billion bushels.

★ CompTrac, a small East Coast construction company in business for less than a decade, was awarded a $40 million contract to build three schools in Saudi Arabia. Winning large contracts seems to be a new trend for small business.

★ It was a great year for animals too. Some residents of Bolton, Massachusetts wanted to limit the number of pigs per farm, claiming that pigs depressed property values. A vote was taken, and the pig supporters won 305 to 195 not to restrict the number of porcine farm residents.

★ The battle to clean up the West River is being won. Species of fish, which even ten years ago could not have survived in the polluted water, are being caught in increasing numbers.

★ The U.S. Postal Service did not raise its rates this year.

★ The New York City Department of Environmental Protection reported that a lot of New Yorkers must have been thoroughly enjoying the final episode of the TV program M*A*S*H. Apparently the water-flow rate increased by 300 million gallons at 11:03 p.m., three minutes after the end of the program. So 1 million New Yorkers waited until the end of the program before using the bathroom.

★ And a final note, the death rate from suicide is going down.

Exercise 1
Find words in the text which mean:
1. an answer to a problem
2. physical imperfections
3. a written agreement
4. people who are in favor of something
5. a group of people working together
6. a sum of money that is lacking in the total amount
7. a period of recuperation
8. people who make laws
9. the collection of fruit, grain, or vegetables made by a farmer
10. a period of ten years

Exercise 2
Find expressions which mean:
1. began to write
2. with no unusual occurrences
3. sponsored by
4. with as little work as possible

Exercise 3
There are five examples of the use of "to win." What are they?

Discussion points.

When a dog bites a man, that is not news, but when a man bites a dog, that is news.

No news is good news.

What do you think these sayings mean? Discuss.
The President said that newspapers always print the bad news. Is that true?
Why do you think newspapers might concentrate on bad news?
Would you buy a newspaper which only reported good news? Why? Why not?
Did you read the news yesterday? What was it? Was it all bad?
Give some examples of good news.

Unit 61

THE COMPANY PICNIC

Every year, the Austin, Texas operation of Orange Computers gives a Fourth of July picnic for all its employees and their families. The picnic is held at a man-made lake near town, and everyone enjoys swimming, water skiing, going out in boats, playing games, and especially eating the big barbecue lunch.

Leslie Carbone works in the Accounting Department. She's talking to Diane Romberg, the Personnel Director.

Leslie: Hi, Diane. Was that your son David you were just talking to?

Diane: Oh hi, Leslie. Yeah, that was David. I don't know what to do with him. He never wants to play with the other kids.

Leslie: He certainly has grown since last year. He's so tall now that I wasn't sure it was him.

Diane: Yeah, he's much taller than most kids his age. Oh, well. How do you like the picnic? Are you having a good time?

Leslie: Oh, yes, great! I—uh—wanted to ask you about that job in the New York office.

Diane: It's definitely opening up. Are you still interested in it?

Leslie: I might be. I really don't know what to do. I'm really happy here in Austin, but it would be nice to be in New York. My family lives in New Jersey. Maybe I'll apply for it.

Diane: Why not? Drop by my office next week and I'll tell you what I can about it. Of course, you have to decide what you want.

Jeff Arnold works in the Shipping Department. He's at the picnic with his wife Helene, who is an independent real estate agent.

Jeff: Come on, Helene, what I want to know is why you have to flirt with Phil every time you see him.

Helene: We were just riding in Kay's boat. There's no need to get jealous.

Jeff: I saw what he was doing! He was whispering in your ear.

Helene: Oh, Jeff, you don't know what you're talking about. He almost had to shout because of the motor. How much beer have you had?

Jeff: What I've had to drink has nothing to do with it.

Helene: Do you want to know what he was saying?

Jeff: I don't care what he said. I . . .

Helene: He was asking me what he should get Lisa for her birthday, that's all.

Jackie Pulido is in charge of the Marketing Department. She's just seen Bart Conners, who works in the Advertising Department.

Bart: Jackie! I see you're back from your trip.

Jackie: Yes, I got in last night.

Bart: How did it go?

Jackie: Fabulous. What I saw over there really surprised me. I think there'll be a lot of demand for our new C2L personal computer.

Bart: That's very interesting.

Jackie: Yes, really. What I found was very encouraging. We have just what they're looking for.

Richard Eng is the Orange Computers Vice-President who is in charge of the Austin operation. He's just run into Bob Ewing, who is the Plant Manager.

Richard: Hi, Bob. It's another good picnic, isn't it?

Bob: Yeah, it really is.

Richard: Did you get my memo about the meeting Wednesday?

Bob: Yeah, 10 o'clock, right? Your memo didn't say what the meeting's about. It's not bad news, is it?

Richard: No, don't worry. It's good news in fact. What we need to do is increase production of the C2L. Either we'll have to go into overtime or hire new people.

Bob: Terrific! What we'll have to look at is how much each way will cost.

Richard: Right, but we can cover the facts and figures on Wednesday. Let's not talk shop today. That's not what we're here for.

Bob: You're right. Have you tried the barbecued ribs?

Kelly Day works in the Inventory Department, and Teresa Guzman works in Data Processing.

Kelly: Hey, Teresa, wasn't that Neil Pincher you were swimming with?

Teresa: He was swimming with me. I wasn't swimming with him.

Kelly: I knew you had better taste.

Teresa: Do you know what he asked me? To go to a movie with him.

Kelly: What did you say?

Teresa: What I wanted to say was, "Buzz off, turkey," but what I said was that I was busy.

Look at this:

I don't know *what* to do with him.
I'll see *what* I can do.
What I saw surprised me.

NEW ON THE JOB

It's Alan Newman's first day on his first job. It's in the Maintenance Department at an electric appliance factory. The Personnel Director, Betty Vaughn, is introducing him to Burt Hogg, who has worked there for twenty-five years.

Betty: Alan, this is Burt Hogg. You'll be working with him.

Alan: Hello, Mr. Hogg.

Burt: Just call me Burt, son. Don't worry. I'll show you what to do.

Betty: I'll leave him with you then, Burt.

Burt: O.K., Betty. I'll look after him. Follow me, son.

Burt: All right, son. Any questions?

Alan: Uh—yeah. Where can I leave my jacket and things?

Burt: There's a row of lockers over there. It doesn't matter which one you use. Take whichever one you want.

Alan: Oh, thanks. And I have my Social Security card. They told me to bring it. Who should I show it to?

Burt: You should have shown it to Betty. I guess she forgot to ask you about it. Just take it up to Personnel. You can show it to whoever is there. They'll pass it on to Betty.

Alan: When can I do that?

Burt: It really doesn't matter. Go whenever you want to, son, but let me give you a tip. Don't go just before lunch or just before closing time. You know what I mean?

Alan: Yeah, right. Thanks.

Alan: Oh, another thing, Burt. Where can I park my motorcycle?

Burt: There's plenty of room in the parking lot. Just don't put it in one of the spaces that are reserved for the department managers and the company officers. Other than that, you can leave it wherever there's room. Come on, I'll show you where you'll be working. In here. That's your workbench, and your stool is here, and over there are the filing cabinets. Just watch me at first and do whatever I tell you, O.K.?

Alan: O.K.

Burt: First of all, you can clean these tools. There's some solvent in that bottle on the shelf.

Alan: All right. Is there any special way to do it?

Burt: Huh? A special way? No, Alan. Clean them however you want to. There's no special way.

10:30

Burt: Ugh! Come on, Alan, you can stop for a while. It's time for a break.

Alan: Thanks.

Burt: Don't thank me, son. You're doing a good job. It's time for a cup of coffee—or whatever you want. Oh, and after the break, I want you to go to the Supply Room and get me a few things, O.K.?

Alan: Sure. I'll get whatever you want.

Burt: Good. I need a can of striped paint, a rubber hammer and a glass nail, a left-handed screwdriver, and a bucket of steam. Just tell them Burt sent you.

At the Supply Room

Alan: Hi there.

Supply Clerk: Hi there.

Alan: I'm here to get a can of striped paint.

Supply Clerk: A what? What are you talking about, boy?

Alan: I was sent here to pick up a can of striped paint.

Supply Clerk: And what wise guy told you to do that, Alan?

Alan: Burt—Burt Hogg.

Supply Clerk: Oh, Burt Hogg. I see. What color stripes would you like?

Alan: Oh. I don't know. Maybe I'd better ask him.

Supply Clerk: I suppose he told you to get a right-handed screwdriver too.

Alan: No, he wants a left-handed one.

Supply Clerk: Think about what you're saying. Just stop and think.

Alan: But Burt said. . . . Oh. Hmmm. Oh, yeah—uh—excuse me.

A few minutes later

Burt: What took you so long, Alan?

Alan: Well, the Supply Room didn't have what you wanted, so I filled out a requisition form and took it to the president's office. You've been here so long that I'm sure he'll approve whatever you want.

Exercise 1

A: What would you like to do tonight?

B: *I don't care—whatever you like.*

1. Well, where would you like to go?
2. How do you want to go there?
3. Which would you rather take—a bus or a taxi?
4. When do you think we should leave?
5. What bar are we going to go to?
6. What do you want?
7. Where do you want to go for dinner?
8. Who should we invite to the party?
9. What should we serve?

Exercise 2

A: What should I do with these old newspapers?

B: *It doesn't matter. Do whatever you want to.*

1. So, which of these books can I borrow?
2. Who should I give my ticket to?
3. When can I come to see you?
4. How should I do it?
5. Where can I park my car?

A CHANGE FOR THE BETTER?

Newspapers and magazines are full of advertisements which try to persuade people to change their appearance in one way or another. Look at these ads and discuss them.

ADVERTISEMENTS

Unit 64

SEEING THE DOCTOR

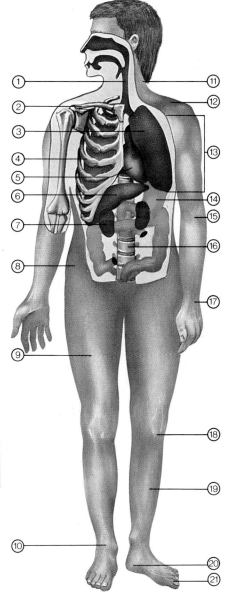

Exercise 1

List as many words as you can about:
a. illness
b. medical treatment
c. parts of the body.
Listen to the conversation and check any words in your list that are used in the conversation.

Craig Williams has gone to see Dr. Casey. He's in her office now.

Mary Healy fell off her bicycle. She's in the emergency room at the local hospital. Dr. Singh is examining her.

Doctor: Well, hello, young lady. It looks like you've had quite a fall. What were you doing? Going too fast?

Mary: Yes, doctor. I fell off going around a corner.

Doctor: I see. Well, let me take a look at you. Hmm. That's a bad cut. I'll have to put a couple of stitches in that.

Mary: I have a cut here too, doctor.

Doctor: It looks worse than it is. Only the skin is broken. The nurse will clean it up for you. It'll sting, but that's all. Now, does it hurt anywhere else?

Mary: I have a pain in my arm. It's very sore, and it feels stiff.

Doctor: Well, there's nothing broken, but you've bruised your shoulder. It'll be sore for a few days. Did you bump your head?

Mary: Yes, I did. I fell on the bike. But it doesn't hurt now.

Doctor: Did you feel dizzy?

Mary: No, not at all.

Doctor: Look up there. I'm going to shine this light in your eye. Uh huh. All right. That's fine. I'll sew this cut up, and the nurse will put a bandage on it. Then you can go home.

Jean Weiner has gone to see Dr. Carlos Valencia, her family doctor.

Jean: Good morning, doctor.

Doctor: Oh, good morning, Mrs. Weiner. What seems to be the problem today?

Jean: It's those pills, doctor. They don't seem to be doing me any good.

Doctor: Really? What's wrong?

Jean: What isn't wrong with me, doctor! It's old age, I suppose.

Doctor: You're doing very well, Mrs. Weiner! You'll live to be a hundred!

Jean: I have this terrible cough, doctor, and I still have that rash on my hands. And the backache! I can hardly walk sometimes. You don't think it's cancer, do you? I've been reading so much about it in the paper.

Doctor: No, no. No chance of that. You're in good shape for your age.

Jean: You can't be serious. Anyway, I'm almost finished with the old pills, doctor. Can you give me a different color next time?

① throat	⑧ hip	⑮ elbow
② collar bone	⑨ thigh	⑯ spine
③ lung	⑩ ankle	⑰ wrist
④ rib	⑪ neck	⑱ knee
⑤ heart	⑫ shoulder	⑲ shin
⑥ liver	⑬ chest	⑳ heel
⑦ kidney	⑭ stomach	㉑ toe

Exercise 2

Rosemary Trabulsi wants to take out a life insurance policy. The insurance company has sent her to see a doctor for a physical examination. This is part of the form that has to be filled out.

Practice their conversation. (*Let me take/measure your.... /Have you ever had ...?/Have you been vaccinated against ...?* etc.)

CONTINENTAL MUTUAL BENEFICIAL INSURANCE CO. Boston

Physical: Form 4F84

Name	Children . . . . '. . .	Address . . . .
Marital status	Occupation	. . . .
Date of birth		

Measurements

Height	Pulse rate	Waist . . . .
Weight	Chest (a) normal	Hips . . . .
Blood pressure	(b) expanded	Eyesight . . . .

Medical history (please give approximate dates where possible)

Measles	**Vaccinations and inoculations**	Please give details of any hospital
Mumps	Polio	treatment or operations (not
Rubella (German measles)	Small pox	including normal pregnancy)
Chicken-pox	Others	
Whooping cough	**Injuries or problems**	. . . .
Other serious illnesses (give	Arms, hands	. . . .
details below)	Back	. . . .
. . . .	Legs, knees	. . . .
. . . .	Internal organs	. . . .

A MESSAGE TO THE STARS

Our planet Earth is one of nine planets revolving around the Sun, a fairly small and ordinary star, which lies in the outer areas of the Milky Way galaxy. There are about 250 billion stars in our galaxy and billions of galaxies in the universe. People have always wondered about the possibility of intelligent life forms on other planets. In recent years this has become serious scientific speculation. Some scientists believe that there must be large numbers of stars with planets which could support living intelligent beings. Perhaps we will never know. The nearest star is 4.3 light years away. A light year is the distance covered by light (traveling at about 186,000 miles a second) in one year. It would take the fastest Earth spacecraft about 40,000 years to reach the nearest star.

For a number of years radio telescopes have been trying to pick up signals from outer space, so far without success. There are, however, millions of possible radio frequencies, and there is no reason why a completely alien civilization should not use a different type of communication, such as X-rays or even a type of wave we have not yet discovered. Suppose contact were made with beings 300 light years away. By the time we had sent our reply and received their response, the earth would be 600 years older. It would be an interesting, but rather slow-moving conversation!

Pioneer 10

The first man-made object to leave our solar system was the Pioneer 10 spacecraft. It was launched from Cape Kennedy on March 3, 1972. It was designed to pass close to the planet Jupiter. In 1983 it left the outer limits of the planetary system. A gold plaque, 6 inches by 9 inches, was placed on the spacecraft. On the plaque is a diagram showing the solar system and its lo-

cation in the galaxy. There is also a drawing of a man and a woman, standing in front of a picture of the spacecraft. The man's right hand is raised in a gesture of friendship. It is unlikely, however, that the plaque will ever be seen again. If it were found by an alien civilization, it seems improbable that they would be able to interpret it.

The Voyager Mission

Every 175 years the large outer planets—Jupiter, Saturn, Uranus, and Neptune—are in such a position that a spacecraft from Earth can fly past all of them. The two Voyager spacecraft were launched in 1977 to photograph and investigate these planets. Voyager I passed Jupiter in December 1978 and reached Saturn in November 1980. It sent back dramatic pictures of the rings of Saturn and discovered previously unknown moons. It then left the solar system. Voyager II was designed to reach Saturn in July 1981, Uranus in January 1986 and Neptune in Au-

gust 1989 before leaving the solar system to travel silently through space. Its next stop—no one knows.

As well as a pictorial plaque, Voyager II carries a gold sprayed disc. The disc contains greetings in 60 languages, 140 photographs, and one and a half hours of music and songs, ranging in style from Beethoven and Mozart to the Beatles and Chuck Berry.

Exercise 1
Imagine you could send objects, weighing up to 10 pounds, which would give an impression of civilization on Earth. This would include a record and a video tape with photographs and film. What would you choose to send and why?

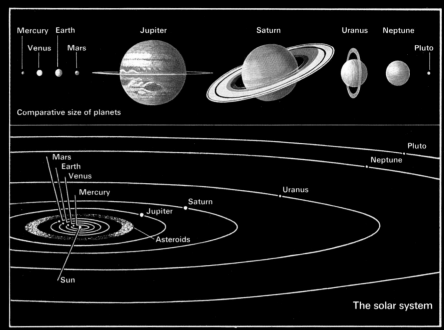

Comparative size of planets

The solar system

Exercise 2
Space research costs billions of dollars. Some people think that the money would be better spent on more practical projects here on Earth. What do you think?

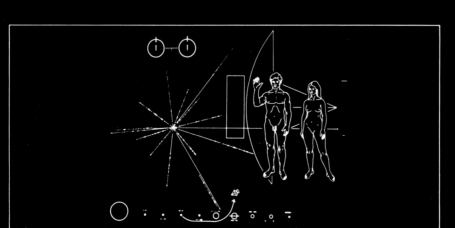

IT'S ABOUT TIME

Janet and Bruce live in Washington, D.C. Janet's younger sister, Pam, who lives in Columbus, Ohio, is flying down to spend a long weekend with them.

Janet: Bruce, I think it's time to go and meet Pam at the airport.
Bruce: Oh, no, there's no need to hurry. There's plenty of time. It's only eight-thirty. There won't be much traffic at this time of night.
Janet: You never know, and I think your watch must be slow. I have 8:40, and we'll have to stop for gas. I'd rather be too early than too late!
Bruce: It'll take her a while to get her luggage.
Janet: Oh, come on, Bruce! It's time we were leaving. We can always have some coffee at the airport. Anyway, I like watching people at the airport.
Bruce: I'd rather see the end of the basketball game, but never mind, we'd better go.

Bruce: Janet! Wait a minute. The phone's ringing.
Janet: We don't have time to answer it now. Ignore it.
Bruce: No, I'd better see who it is. It might be important.. Hello? . . . Oh, Pam, we were just on our way to pick you up. . . . Oh, no! Hold on, I'll put Janet on the phone.

Janet: Hi, Pam! Where are you?
Pam: I'm still in Columbus. The flight's been delayed.
Janet: You caught us just in time. We

were just about to leave for the airport.
Pam: I know, that's what Bruce said. I'm glad I called. You would have had a long wait otherwise.
Janet: When will you be leaving, do you think?
Pam: Oh, not for another hour at least. Look, don't bother to come out to the airport.
Janet: It's no trouble. We'll meet you.
Pam: No, I'd really rather you didn't. Honestly.
Janet: Now, don't be silly, Pam. We'll pick you up.
Pam: No, Janet, I'd rather get a taxi.
Janet: We'll be there, Pam! See you later.

Janet: Oh, Bruce, there she is!
Bruce: It's about time.
Janet: Pam! Pam! Over here!
Pam: Janet! Bruce! Mmm. It's wonderful to see you, but I'm really embarrassed. It's nearly 12:30.
Janet: Well, we couldn't let you find your own way—not at this time of night.
Bruce: Do we have to wait for the luggage or is that all you have?
Pam: No, this is it. I didn't check anything.
Bruce: Great! It always takes forever and a day at this airport.
Janet: I know. It's about time they did something about it. Last time it took me longer than the flight.

Bruce: I'll go and get the car. I won't take long.
Janet: Well, Pam, what would you

rather do tomorrow morning, sleep in or go shopping?
Pam: You mean this morning! I'd rather go shopping, but there's no need for you to get up and come with me. I'd rather let you sleep in. You must be exhausted!
Janet: I am a little tired, and Bruce is too. But I'll meet you for lunch. There's a new restaurant just down the street from Woodwind & Loafop. Do you think you'll be able to find it?
Pam: Oh, Janet! It isn't as if this were my first time in Washington! You can tell me where it is in the morning.

Look at this:

I'd	rather	go there.	
I'd	rather	you	went there.
		he	didn't go there.
		she	
		we	
		they	

It's (about) time	to go	
	we left.	
	we were leaving.	

It isn't as	if	this were my first visit.
	though	he didn't know.

Exercise 1
The baggage handling is slow. They should do something about it.
It's about time they did something about it.
Continue.
1. It's late. We should go to the airport.
2. She's getting tired. She should go to bed.
3. He coughs a lot. He should stop smoking.
4. The windows are dirty. We should clean them.
5. The bus is late. It should be here.
6. He's bored. He should find an interesting job.

Exercise 2
Are you going to do it?
No, I'd rather not do it. I'd rather you did it.
Continue.
1. Are you going to write to her?
2. Would you like to drive?
3. Do you want to ask him?
4. Would you like to choose?
5. Do you want to arrange it?
6. Are you going to see the manager?

THE NEW YORK POLICE FORCE

"Thanks for inviting me to speak at your career assembly. You've asked me to talk about what it's like being a police officer. Well, I'm going to be honest with you. It's a rough profession, and you have to be sure it's what you really want to do. It's no picnic being a police officer in New York City. When people need your help, they're only too happy to call you. But just you show up when they don't want you and what you can get called isn't fit to print. It's one of the few occupations left in present-day society where a person can arrive for work and have no idea what the day will bring. It could be a traffic accident or a murder, an armed robbery or a false alarm, a request for directions or a drug overdose. I get asked about vacations, treatment for sick canaries, social security, ecology, contraception, politics, and prison visits. I have to deal with family abuse—battered children, injured wives, abused husbands. I get anonymous threatening letters and phone calls and a lot of times I recognize who they're from. I get invited to christenings, weddings, and divorces—and often in that order, particularly with young people. I rarely complete a holiday shift, especially Christmas, without having to report a suicide, usually caused by loneliness. Every day there are drunks, fights, bodies, demonstrations, the brutal and the brave, the villains and the victims, the haters and the lovers,

and the just plain indifferent. It isn't easy.

Any police officer in New York could tell you a similar story. But the question it would raise is the same. What kind of person measures up to such a job? Any one of you. There's no minimum height requirement—you can be tall or short. But regardless of your height you're obviously no good if you don't have the stature for the job. This means having concern for people, a real sense of fair play. And if you don't have a sense of humor, forget it. These qualities are more important than qualifications, although you need some of those too. You have to be a high school graduate and at least 20 years old to get into the Police Academy, but you can take the exams before you're 20. And those exams are tough. First you have to pass a written exam. They want to find out if you've got common sense. If you make it through that, you have to take a physical exam, and you'd better be in good shape. Then you need a medical exam. If you pass that, you go to the Police Academy for six months. And the pay starts at $22,000 a year. But believe me, you'll earn every penny of it. Violent criminals, horrible accidents, and freezing weather will turn up when you least expect them. You'll have to put up with lonely hours on the night shift and you'll probably work every Christmas.

But the reward you can get as a human being for doing a good job will more than compensate for the low pay. If I haven't dimmed your enthusiasm and you're still interested, you can do two things. First read a few books written by ex-cops. They'll tell you plenty. One is called *Police in Blue.* If that doesn't give you the truth, nothing will. And also get in touch with the Department of Personnel, 55 Thomas Street, New York, NY. Or call them at (212) 566-8790. They'll tell you when the next exam is being given.

Thanks a lot. And good luck."

GOLD

Gold (Au) is a metallic chemical element. Atomic number 79. Atomic weight 197.2.

Since civilization began, gold has been regarded as a symbol of power and wealth. In many societies gold was seen as a magic substance which could protect people against illness or evil spirits. It is the one material that has always been accepted in exchange for goods or services. Humanity never seems to have enough gold, and the search for it has driven people crazy. The need to search for gold has been compared to a disease and is called "gold fever." In the Middle Ages people called "alchemists" tried to manufacture gold from other metals. In spite of the constant search for gold, the amount which has been produced since the beginning of time is only enough to make a solid block of eighteen cubic meters, the size of a large house.

Industrial Uses

Because gold is untarnishable, workable, almost indestructible, durable, reflective, and conductive, it has a number of industrial uses. About 10% of the annual production is used for industrial processes.
• Gold is measured in troy ounces (31.1 grams). One ounce can be drawn into 50 miles (about 80 km) of wire. A single grain (0.065 grams) can be beaten down to make a sheet which would cover this page.
• Between 20 and 30 ounces are needed for every jet engine. Gold coatings, 0.000024 mm thick, are used to reflect heat from jet engine exhausts.
• The windhsields of the Concorde, other high speed aircraft, and some express trains have a gold electric heating element, 0.000005 mm thick, which is used to prevent icing.
• Spacecraft are protected against radiation by a thin layer of the metal.
• Because it conducts electricity well and does not tarnish, gold is used extensively in computers and electric consumer products.

• For many years it has been blended with oils and applied as decoration to china and glass.
• Because it is so reflective, it is employed in the manufacture of some roof tiles and glass.
• Gold has always been prescribed for various ailments, and it is used today to treat cancer and arthritis. It is also used extensively in dentistry.

Decorative Purposes

Because gold is valuable, bright, rare, attractive, durable, and untarnishable it has always been used for decorative purposes. Gold works of art were created by many of the great civilizations of the past and may be seen in museums all over the world.
• Since time immemorial gold has been coveted and desired. Until recent years it was worn only by the very rich and was considered the ultimate status symbol.
• Gold jewelry is generally made to three standards: 22, 18, and 14 carats. 18 carat gold is 18 parts gold out of 24, which is pure gold. That is, 18 carats is 75% pure gold. 24 carat gold is too soft for most purposes.
• Gold jewelry includes rings, earrings, necklaces, bracelets, chains, pendants, armlets, anklets, medals, cufflinks, tie pins, eyeglass frames, and watches. It is also used to decorate pens, lighters, drinking glasses, and books.
• In traditional Indian cooking, gold flakes are used to decorate food and are consumed.

Financial Uses

The first gold coin was issued by King Croesus of Lydia in the sixth century B.C. Today gold still plays an important part in the international monetary system. About thirty years' worth of gold production is being held by central banks and monetary authorities, in spite of efforts to reduce its importance.
• New deposits of gold are being found, and old mines are being reopened. It is likely that gold will always be valued as protection against inflation.
• Gold can be bought by private investors in the form of bars, coins, and medals, as well as jewelry.

Gold Production

Gold is found on all five continents, but 85% of the annual output of gold is produced by four countries:

South Africa	30 million oz.
USSR	5½ million oz.
Canada	4 million oz.
USA	1½ million oz.

In South Africa about three tons of gold-bearing rock have to be mined to produce each ounce of gold. Billions of tons of gold are suspended in the oceans, but this gold is impossible to exploit at the present time.

Look at this:
Gold *is used* for many purposes.
It *was produced* in ancient times.
Gold *has been used* for 6000 years.
New deposits *are being* found.
It *will be valued* in the future.
It *can be used* in industrial processes.
It *may be seen* in museums.
Three tons of rock *have to be mined* to produce an ounce of gold.

GOLD RUSH!

California

In 1848 gold was discovered at Sutter's Mill, about 100 miles east of San Francisco, and the first great gold rush began. When the news leaked out, farmers, trappers, lawyers, preachers, sailors, soldiers, and school teachers rushed to California by whatever means they could. Within a year 100,000 people, only 8,000 of whom were women, had reached the coast of California. More than half of them had traveled overland across the American continent. "Gold fever" began to spread. Settlements throughout the United States were deserted. Homes, farms, and stores were abandoned as everybody raced for California. Many came by sea, and in July, 1850 more than 500 ships were anchored in San Francisco Bay, many of which had been deserted by gold-hungry sailors. A few people became fabulously rich, but it was a risky business. Law and order broke down. Even if a miner "struck it rich" there were always those who would try to take it away: gamblers, outlaws, thieves, and saloon keepers. Gold and silver were discovered in Nevada a few years later, and "gold fever" was an important part of the settlement of the western United States.

Australia

The next major gold rush occurred in 1851, when gold was struck in New South Wales, Australia. This led to another stampede, and many rich finds were made. Other discoveries were made in Victoria and Kalgoorlie, Western Australia. In some places massive nuggets of gold were found accidentally, just lying about on the ground. The "Welcome Stranger" nugget, which was found in 1869, weighed almost 173 pounds (78.37 kilos).

The Yukon

Perhaps the most difficult conditions were experienced by those prospectors who braved the Canadian winters to win gold from the Yukon and Klondike rivers. On August 16th, 1896 three prospectors struck gold in Bonanza Creek, a tributary of the Klondike River, and then in a second creek which was named "Eldorado." In the Yukon, gold was obtained by washing gravel from river-beds, and soon as much as $800 worth of gold was being taken from a single pay of dirt. Within a year, Dawson had grown from nothing to a town of 30,000 people. Everybody who entered the country had to carry a year's supply of food and mining equipment over steep and frozen mountain passes. To do this, each prospector had to carry 55 pounds (25 kilos) of stores about 6 miles (10 km), leave it there, and return for another load. Therefore, to move all their stores 50 miles (80 km), people had to walk nearly 940 miles (about 1500 km). Horses and donkeys died in the ice and snow, but the people kept on going. It is estimated that of the 100,000 people who set out for the Klondike, fewer than 40,000 actually arrived. Only 4000 ever found gold, and very few of these became rich.

The rising price of gold in the late 1970s started a new rush to the Klondike. Dawson is still there, and "Diamond Tooth Gertie's," the only legal gambling hall in Canada, is still in business. Just outside Dawson, a mountain is actually being moved to find gold. The whole mountain is being washed down for gold dust. It is believed to contain at least $80 million worth of gold.

South Africa

By the turn of the century gold had been found in South Africa, and this laid the foundation for the world's largest gold mining industry. Today South Africa accounts for 70% of world gold production. Vast sums of money are being invested, and modern mining technology is being used to squeeze gold from the rock.

Twentieth Century Gold Rush

New finds are being made in the Soviet Union, Saudi Arabia, and the United States. The largest single mine in the world was discovered in Uzbekistan, USSR, in 1958. However, in spite of recent finds, modern day "gold rushes" are usually confined to speculation on the gold markets of Zurich, London, and New York. At times of economic uncertainty investors rush hysterically to buy gold, and the price soars, often only to fall back again. Gold fever is in many ways irrational, but historically gold has always held its value, and it is likely that in an uncertain world it will continue to do so.

Look at these expressions. What do you think they might mean?

The golden rule.
A golden age.
A golden boy.
The golden gates.
A golden wedding anniversary.
A golden opportunity.
As good as gold.
Everything he touches turns to gold (or He's got the Midas touch).
All that glitters is not gold.
Don't kill the goose that lays the golden eggs.
A heart of gold.
A gold digger.
A gold medal.
Go for gold.
A goldbrick.

THE CIRCUS IS COMING

John: Good morning. This is "What's New," Portstown, Delaware's favorite radio talk show. I'm your host, John Barca. In the studio with me is Sandy Farnham, the daughter of famous circus owner T. P. Farnham. Sandy, the circus will be here in Portstown for two weeks. That's right, isn't it?

Sandy: Yes, that's right, John. We open tomorrow for two weeks.

John: Has the circus arrived yet, Sandy?

Sandy: No, John, not yet. It's on the road somewhere between New Jersey and here.

John: I suppose there's a lot to be done between now and the first show.

Sandy: Yes, that's right. I've already been here for three days. There were all the advance arrangements to be made. It's like preparing for a small invasion, I guess you could say.

John: What do you mean?

Sandy: Well, there are so many things to be done, you know. There are posters to be put up, newspaper ads to be arranged, local workers to be hired. It goes on and on.

John: When will the circus actually arrive?

Sandy: In the next hour or two. The first trucks should be arriving any minute now, and then the hard work really begins.

John: Most people love the circus. But not many realize how much work there is, do they?

Sandy: That's right. We'll be working all day and most of the night. It's a lot like moving a small army. But, I'm keeping my fingers crossed. By tomorrow morning everything will have been set up in time for the afternoon performance. But first there's the big parade down Main Street at 11:30. Don't forget to come out and see us.

John: Thank you, Sandy, for coming in to talk to us. Now don't forget, folks. The big circus parade will start from the pier at 11:30, go along Main Street past the high school, and end in Lincoln Park. Farnham's Circus will be in town for two weeks until August 28th. Now for our next guest . . .

Exercise 1

This is Sandy's checklist of arrangements:

1. consult police about parking
   (Portstown Police Department)
2. arrange telephone lines
   (Delaware Telephone Company)
3. connect water supply
   (Portstown Department of Sanitation)
4. place ads
   (*Portstown Echo, Delaware Press,* Portstown Radio Station WPTD)
5. order food supplies for animals
   (Dover Meat Company)
6. arrange for fire protection
   (Portstown Fire Department)

All of these things will have been done before the circus arrives. Make sentences.

A telephone line will have been arranged.
She'll have contacted the Delaware Telephone Company.

Exercise 2

Sandy's brother, Eddie Farnham, is in charge of the menagerie. This is his checklist:

1. unload animals
2. collect meat supplies
3. water animals
4. feed animals
5. check sanitary arrangments for the animals
6. provide straw for animals

The animals have to be unloaded.
Make sentences.

Exercise 3

It's eleven o'clock on Sunday morning. There's a lot to be done. Sandy's father, T. P. Farnham, is in charge of the arrangements.

1. erect big top
2. set up ticket office
3. park wagons
4. put up stands
5. erect cages
6. connect generators
7. put up safety net
8. set up tightrope
9. put up trapezes
10. set up bandstand
11. place loudspeakers in tent
12. connect amplifiers
13. set up and connect lights
14. connect microphones
15. check everything

There's the big top to be erected.
Make sentences.

GETTING THINGS DONE

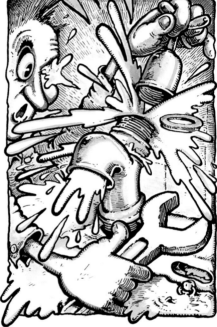

Anne: Tim! That bathroom faucet is still dripping. It's driving me crazy! I thought you said you were going to fix it.

Tim: Oh, yeah. The washer needs replacing.

Anne: Why don't you replace it then?

Tim: That's easier said than done. I'll try and do it next week.

Anne: But you said that last week.

Tim: I know. I think you'd better call a plumber and get it done. I'm not really sure how to do it. I'm sorry, Mom.

Exercise 1
Make conversations using the following:
1. that light's still broken/socket/electrician
2. the brake lights on my car aren't working/bulb/take it to a garage
3. the turntable sounds terrible/stylus/take it to a repair shop
4. one of the burners on the stove isn't working/heating element/electrician
5. the reception on this TV set is very poor/antenna/TV repairman

Mark and Tiffany are going on vacation next week. They're driving to Las Vegas. Mark always gives Tiffany a lift to work. He's dropping her off outside her office.

Mark: Oh, Tiffany! I won't be able to pick you up from work tonight. I'm having the car tuned up. I thought we'd better have it done before we go.

Tiffany: Good idea. No problem. When are you picking it up?

Mark: Not till quarter to six. Why?

Tiffany: Well, I want to have my hair done before we leave. I'll try and make an appointment to get it done after work. Then you can pick me up at the hairdresser's.

Mark: O.K. Can you call me at work and let me know what time?

Tiffany: All right, I'll call you later. Bye.

Exercise 2

TIPS FOR VACATION DRIVERS
Before leaving on a long trip, don't forget to:
- ☞ have a complete tune-up
- ☞ change the oil
- ☞ check the battery
- ☞ test the brakes
- ☞ check the tires carefully and
- ☞ change or rotate if necessary

Mark *doesn't have* time to do any of these things himself.
He's going to have the car tuned up.
Make five more sentences.

Exercise 3
Tiffany's going to have her hair done.
Make sentences with:
wash/shampoo/trim/dye/cut/perm

Exercise 4

HOUSES FOR SALE
Quaint farmhouse. Built 1872. 3 bedrooms. Handyman's special. Needs work. Outdoor plumbing. Ideal for roughing it or for do-it-yourself enthusiast. Very reasonable price. Uciardi & Cotten Real Estate Agency, Concord. (603) 689-1242.

Look at the ad for a farm house in New Hampshire. It is old and in very bad condition. Imagine you were interested in buying it. What do you think might need to be done?

The house might need repainting.
Make a list.

Exercise 5
Listen to the conversation between a real estate agent and Robin and Gene Harvey, who are looking at the house. Check any items on your list that are mentioned in the conversation.

Exercise 6
When Robin and Gene are talking about the house, they mention some things that they could do themselves and some things they would have to have done. Look at the chart below and the example: They would have to have kitchen units and major appliances put in. Listen to the conversation again and complete the chart.

	Do it themselves	Have it done by someone else
Put in kitchen units and major appliances		✓
Install plumbing for modern kitchen		
Put down vinyl tiles on floor		
Rewire house		
Put in more electrical outlets		
Cover all walls with sheet rock		
Paint all walls and ceilings		
Convert small bedroom into bathroom		
Install bath and toilet plumbing		
Repair roof		
Put in new oil burner		
Weatherproof windows		
Put in insulation		

What could you do yourself, and what would you have done by someone else?

GETTING IN SHAPE

MONDAY, OCTOBER 16, 1983

14,546 Win Marathon
Millions Watch World's Biggest Sporting Event
by Dennis Stone

QUESTIONNAIRE

1. Would you describe yourself as:
   ☐ Very fit   ☐ Average
   ☐ Pretty fit   ☐ Unfit
   Do you think physical fitness is important?
   ☐ Yes   ☐ No

2. ☐ Do you ever get out of breath?
   ☐ Can you touch your toes (without bending your knees)?
   ☐ Can you run for half a mile?
   ☐ Can you hang from a bar, supporting your own weight for 20 seconds?

3. Does your daily routine involve any physical exertion?
   ☐ Yes   ☐ No

4. Do you exercise regularly?
   ☐ Yes   ☐ No

5. If you exercise regularly, how often do you do it?
   ☐ Every day   ☐ More than once a week
   ☐ Every other day   ☐ Once a week   ☐ Less

6. If you exercise regularly, how do you do it?
   ☐ Sports   ☐ Dance   ☐ Yoga
   ☐ Jogging   ☐ Bicycling   ☐ Walking
   ☐ Swimming   ☐ Indoor exercises
   ☐ Other (What other ways? ....)

7. If you participate in sports, is your favorite sport
   ☐ A team game   ☐ Amateur
   ☐ Competitive   ☐ Professional
   ☐ Organized

8. Do you own any sports equipment?
   ☐ Yes   ☐ No
   If so, what? ....

9. Do you/Did you have to participate in sports at school/college?
   ☐ Yes   ☐ No
   If so, which ones? ....
   How often? ....

10. Do you/did you have Phys. Ed. (Physical Education) classes at school/college?
    ☐ Yes   ☐ No

11. Do you think sports or physical education should be a compulsory part of the school curriculum? college?
    ☐ Yes   ☐ No

12. Why?/Why not? ....

Here are instructions for two fitness exercises:

Warm-up exercise
Stand with the feet apart and the arms out at shoulder level. Bend forward, twisting the torso at the same time to touch the right hand to the left foot. Stand upright again with the arms out and then bend forward and twist touching the left hand to the right foot. Repeat 10 times on each side the first day and gradually increase to 20 repetitions on each side.

Twisting sit-ups
Lie on your back with the legs bent at the knees. You can put the feet under a chair or have someone hold your feet down. Place the hands behind the head. Sit up, twisiting at the same time to bring the right elbow to the outside of the left knee. Lie on your back again. Then sit up and touch the left elbow to the outside of the right knee. Repeat 5 times on each side.

If you do exercises, describe how to do them in detail. Get someone to follow your instructions. If you participate in sports, describe your favorite sport and briefly explain the rules, without mentioning the name of the sport. See if people can guess which sport you have described.

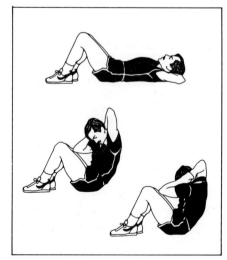

Over 2 million spectators watched yesterday's New York Marathon, the world's largest sporting event, which turned out to have 14,546 winners.

That is the number that finished out of 16,988 who officially started in the Marathon and were cheered as they ran through the streets of all five boroughs of the city. The runners came from all 50 states of the U.S., plus the District of Columbia and Puerto Rico, as well as 68 foreign countries.

The first and last to complete the 26 miles and 385 yards symbolized in their different ways the spirit of the occasion.

In the lead, George O'Doud from Ireland and Inge Simonsen from Norway linked hands to run the last few yards and staged a dead heat for first place.

"What does it matter who wins?" said 33-year-old O'Doud. "Every runner who finishes this race is a winner." Some two hours later, the last one home was the oldest competitor, 84-year-old Bob Vann of Silver City, Colorado. "I feel good. It's great to be alive," he said.

The leaders made it an event of the highest athletic quality. At 2 hours, 8 minutes, 59 seconds, the joint winners ran the fastest Marathon ever — and 142 runners finished under 2 hours 30 minutes.

Race director Fred Lebowitz said: "It went like a dream."

Medical crews under the direction of Dr. Yolanda Rodrigo treated hundreds of runners for exhaustion, but the worst damage reported was a broken leg. "We are surprised there weren't more casualties — everyone was very fit," Dr. Rodrigo said.

The drizzly conditions were ideal for marathon running, and competitors praised the camaraderie of those taking part, and the encouragement that the spectators gave them.

This aspect was summed up by 29-year-old jogger Doris Crowley, from Boston. Four miles from the finish she was on the point of quitting after stumbling to a halt.

Then, she said, she heard the crowd yelling out her number. "No one has ever cheered like that for me before," she said. "They gave me the strength to go on."

DON'T PANIC

1. Don't forget to fasten your seat belts!
2. Please do not leave your seat while the seat belt light is on.
3. May we remind passengers to read the emergency procedures.
4. Please do not smoke in the aisles or in the rest rooms.

5. Would you like to see the cockpit?

6. I'm busy now, but I'll bring you a drink in a minute.

7. I'm afraid I can't sell you another drink, sir.

8. Here's the headset. Let me help you.

9. Please keep your seat belts fastened. We're going through turbulence.

10. Don't panic!

11. Take off your shoes and proceed immediately to the emergency exits.

12. Come on. You can make it! Just slide down the chute.

13. I'll have to push you.

Exercise 1

1. remind
She reminded them to fasten their seat belts.
2. warn
She warned them not to leave their seats.

Continue:
3. remind	**9.** tell
4. tell	**10.** warn
5. invite	**11.** instruct
6. promise	**12.** urge
7. refuse	**13.** force
8. help	

Exercise 2

Look at these sentences.
1. He said, "No, no . . . please don't shoot me."
2. She said, "Whatever you do, don't go to that dentist."
3. He said, "If I were you, I'd travel by train."
4. She said, "Would you like to come to a party on Saturday?"
5. She said, "Don't forget to go to the bank today."
6. The policeman said, "Turn off the engine, and get out of the car."
7. The old man said, "Certainly not. I won't sell it at that price."
8. She said, "Don't worry. I'll definitely meet you at six o'clock."
9. The attendant said, "Would you mind moving your car?"
10. She said, "I'm too busy now. Call back later."

1. *He begged her not to shoot him.*

Continue, using these words:
warn/advise/invite/remind/order/refuse/promise/ask/tell.

Exercise 3

Practice with a partner (one of you is Student A, the other is Student B).

Student A	Student B
Ask B to meet you tonight.	Promise to meet A.
Advise B not to eat so much.	Tell A to mind his/her own business.
Ask B to write a letter from your dictation.	Ask A to speak more slowly.
Invite B to a party.	Refuse politely.
Order B to be quiet.	Tell A not to talk like that.
Remind B to repay the money you lent him/her.	Promise to pay tomorrow.
Threaten to kill B.	Beg A not to do it.
Order B to jump out of the window.	Tell A not to be so silly.
Warn B not to go over the speed limit.	Tell A to watch out for the police!

MESSAGES

Rosa Sampson is a secretary at Standard Security Systems. Her boss, Peter Danieli was away on business on Monday. She took several messages for him. Listen to the conversations and look at the notes.

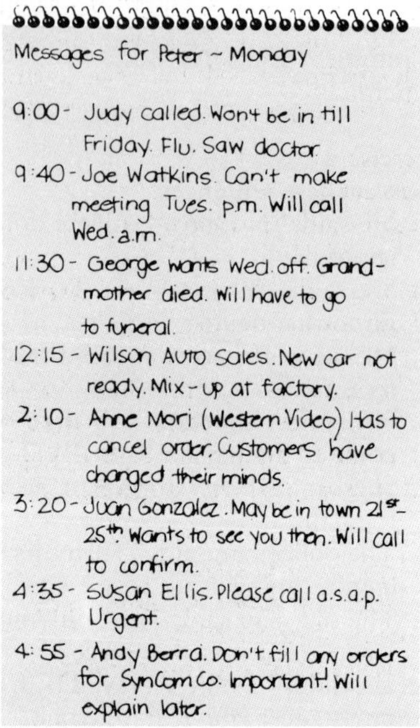

Messages for Peter ~ Monday

9:00 - Judy called. Won't be in till Friday. Flu. Saw doctor

9:40 - Joe Watkins. Can't make meeting Tues. p.m. Will call Wed. a.m.

11:30 - George wants Wed. off. Grandmother died. Will have to go to funeral.

12:15 - Wilson Auto Sales. New car not ready. Mix-up at factory.

2:10 - Anne Mori (Western Video) Has to cancel order. Customers have changed their minds.

3:20 - Juan Gonzalez. May be in town 21st-25th. Wants to see you then. Will call to confirm.

4:35 - Susan Ellis. Please call a.s.a.p. Urgent.

4:55 - Andy Berra. Don't fill any orders for SynCom Co. Important! Will explain later.

It's Tuesday morning. Peter Danieli has just returned to the office after his one-day business trip to Chicago. Look at the notes and listen to Rosa's report.

Peter: Good morning, Rosa. Could you come in for a minute, please?
Rosa: Good morning, Peter. Did you have a good trip?
Peter: Yes, thanks. It went very well.
Rosa: You had quite a few messages yesterday. Should I run through them?
Peter: Yes, go ahead.
Rosa: O.K. Judy called. She said she wouldn't be in till Friday.
Peter: Oh? Why is that?
Rosa: She said she had the flu. She'd seen a doctor.
Peter: O.K. What else?
Rosa: Then Joe Watkins called. He said he couldn't make the meeting this afternoon but would call you on Wednesday morning.
Peter: O.K.
Rosa: George came in looking for you. He said he wanted tomorrow off.
Peter: Did he say why?
Rosa: Yes. He told me his grandmother had died and he'd have to go to the funeral.

Peter: Oh, I'm sorry to hear that. I'd better talk to him later on.
Rosa: And Wilson Auto Sales called. They said your new car wouldn't be ready this week.
Peter: Not again!
Rosa: They said there was a mix-up at the factory.
Peter: That's the second time I've heard that excuse.
Rosa: After lunch Anne Mori called. She said that Western Video Systems had to cancel their last order because their customers had changed their minds.
Peter: Rosa, what about the good news???
Rosa: Let me see ... Juan Gonzalez called from Mexico to say he might be in town from the 21st to the 25th. He said he wanted to see you then and would call to confirm it.
Peter: Good. I hope he can make it.
Rosa: Then a woman called ... Susan Ellis. She asked you to call her as soon as possible. She said it was urgent.
Peter: I wonder what she wants ...
Rosa: Oh, and just before five, Andy Berra called. He told us not to fill any more orders for the SynCom Company until further notice. He said it was important and that he would explain later.
Peter: Anything else?
Rosa: No, that's it.
Peter: Thanks.

Look at this:

Exercise
Joe Taylor is the administrative assistant to Lisa Bates, who is the head buyer for E. Baltman's, a chain of department stores. Lisa was away yesterday visiting a dress manufacturer in Boston. Joe took these messages.

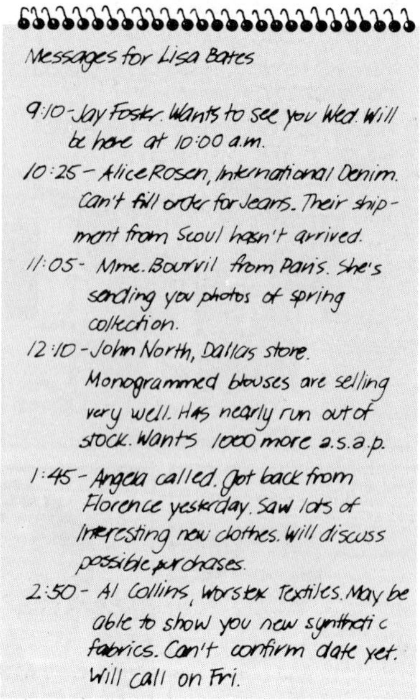

Messages for Lisa Bates

9:10 - Jay Foster. Wants to see you Wed. Will be here at 10:00 a.m.

10:25 - Alice Rosen, International Denim. Can't fill order for jeans. Their shipment from Seoul hasn't arrived.

11:05 - Mme. Bourvil from Paris. She's sending you photos of spring collection.

12:10 - John North, Dallas store. Monogrammed blouses are selling very well. Has nearly run out of stock. Wants 1000 more a.s.a.p.

1:45 - Angela called. Got back from Florence yesterday. Saw lots of interesting new clothes. Will discuss possible purchases.

2:50 - Al Collins, Worstex Textiles. May be able to show you new synthetic fabrics. Can't confirm date yet. Will call on Fri.

Joe reported the messages to Lisa.
9:10 *Jay Foster called. He said he wanted to see you on Wednesday and that he would be here at ten o'clock.*
Report the other messages.

am/is → was	"It's important." She said (that) it was important.
are → were	"They're going to be late." She said (that) they were going to be late.
have/has → had	"I've done the letters." She said (that) she had done the letters.
don't → didn't	"I don't know." She said (that) she didn't know.
want → wanted	"I want a day off." She said (that) she wanted a day off.
didn't do → hadn't done	"I didn't finish it." She said (that) she hadn't finished it.
saw → had seen	"I saw him." She said (that) she had seen him.
was/were → had been	"I wasn't there." She said (that) she hadn't been there.
will/won't → would/wouldn't	"I won't do it." She said (that) she wouldn't do it.
can/can't → could/couldn't	"I can't do it." She said (that) she couldn't do it.
may → might	"I may do it." She said (that) she might do it.

had done/would/could/should/ought/might	No change.

When you are reporting, you may also need to change these words:

this → that
these → those
here → there
now → then
yesterday → the day before
tomorrow → the next day
this (week) → that (week)
last (month) → the (month) before
next (year) → the next (year)

A FEW QUESTIONS

Harry: Who's there?

Ryan: Police. Open up!

Harry: Uh . . . hold on a minute. I'm in the bathroom.

Ryan: Come on! Open up!

Harry: Oh, Lieutenant Ryan. What can I do for you? Is this a social visit?

Ryan: Very funny, Harry. I have a few questions to ask you. Can I come in for a minute?

Harry: Do you have a search warrant?

Ryan: No. Why? Do I need one? Do you have anything to hide, Harry?

Harry: No, no. Nothing at all. Come in. Questions, you said. Well, fire away.

Ryan: Just a routine check, Harry. That's all. Just a routine check. Were you on Sawmill Road last night?

Harry: No.

Ryan: Uh huh. I see. Have you been there recently?

Harry: No. No, I haven't. Why? Has there been any trouble?

Ryan: I'll ask the questions, Harry. Where were you last night?

Harry: I was at the Inner Circle, that new place on Watt Street.

Ryan: Did anybody see you?

Harry: Oh, yes. I have plenty of witnesses.

Ryan: Witnesses, Harry? You haven't been accused of anything—yet. Why do you need witnesses?

Harry: I don't, Lieutenant. I don't. Uh . . . I was with some of my friends.

Ryan: I didn't know you had any, Harry. Who were they?

Harry: Uh, let me think . . . Tommy Ferretti, Al Cohen, and . . .

Ryan: What, Al "The Boot?" I thought he was still inside.

Harry: No, they let him out last week. He got two years off for good behavior. Oh, yeah, Sid Parker was there too.

Ryan: What time did you get there, and what time did you leave?

Harry: I suppose I got there about eight and left at closing time at one.

Ryan: Did you come right home?

Harry: Yeah.

Ryan: How did you get here? Did you drive?

Harry: Oh, no. I'd had a few drinks. I'd never drive under the influence of alcohol, Mr. Ryan. You know me. "Think before you drink before you drive." That's what I always say.

Ryan: Very good, Harry, very good. By the way, is that your car outside? The red Trans Am?

Harry: That's right. I've got all the papers. I can prove it's mine.

Ryan: Nice car. Especially since you're out of work.

Harry: Oh, yeah. Well, my grandmother died. Left me some money.

Ryan: I see. You don't mind me asking, do you?

Harry: Not at all. I mean, that's your job, isn't it?

Ryan: Well, how did you get that dent in the front fender, then?

Harry: Oh. It happened in a parking lot. I wasn't there. Someone must have run into it.

Ryan: That's too bad, Harry. Well, I'll be seeing you. That's all—for now.

Tommy: Yeah!

Harry: Tommy, listen. It's me, Harry.

The police have just been here. It was Ryan again. I don't think he knows anything, but he asked a lot of questions. Uh . . . I told him I was with you.

Tommy: You idiot! Did you have to mention me?

Harry: I'm sorry, Tommy, really I am. Look, we'd better check the details in case they come to see you.

Tommy: What do you mean, "in case they come to see me?" Knowing Ryan, he'll be here any minute. Quick, Harry. Tell me exactly what he asked you, and what you told him.

Exercise 1

"Can I come in for a minute?"
He asked if he could come in, so I asked him if he had a search warrant.
"Where were you last night?"
He asked me where I'd been, and I told him I'd been at the Inner Circle.
Look at the conversation between Harry and Lieutenant Ryan. Report all the questions and answers.

Look at this:

"What's your name?"
She asked me what my name was.
"Are you disturbed?"
She asked me if I was disturbed.

Exercise 2

At Westenberg University's English Language Institute, students who want to take an examination preparation course have to pass a test and have a short interview, to show the ELI administration that their English is good enough to take the course. This is the form which the examiner uses during the interview.

Practice with a partner; one is a student, the other is the examiner.

Examiner: *What's your name?*

Student: *My name's. . . .*

Westenberg University
English Language Institute
Pre-Entry Interview for TOEFL Exam Prep Course

1. Name?
2. Nationality?
3. Hometown?
4. Brothers and sisters?
5. Years of English?
6. Reasons for learning English?
7. Exams passed (if any)?
8. Other languages?
9. Occupation? Tell me about it.
10. Hobbies? Tell me about them.
11. Living arrangements—dormitory, apartment or other?
12. What would you do if you won $50,000?
13. Length of time at Westenberg U.?
14. What do you think about Westenberg?
15. What major differences have you noticed between your social life here and your social life in your hometown?

Exercise 3

Imagine you are a student who has just had the interview. Report to a friend.

Friend: *What did they ask you?*

Student: *They asked me if I had any brothers or sisters. I told them I had one brother and two sisters.*

TRUST THE HEART

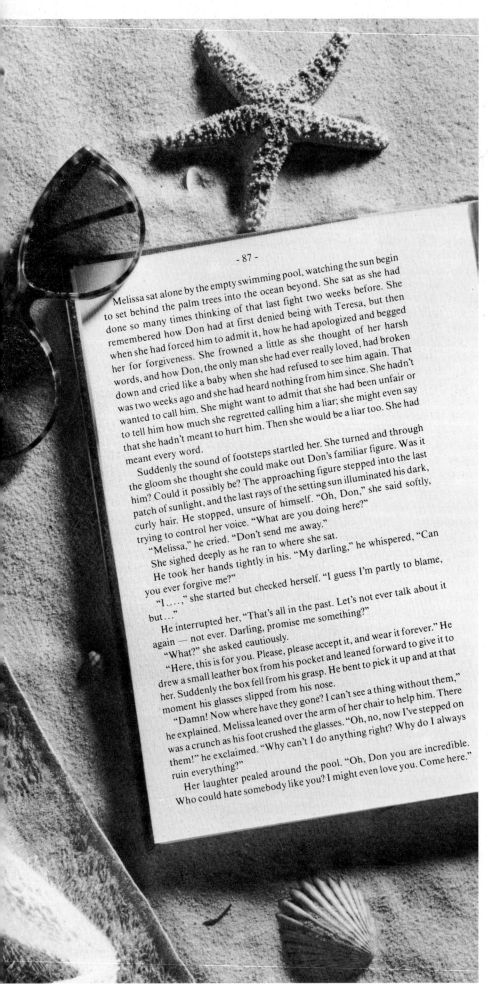

- 87 -

Melissa sat alone by the empty swimming pool, watching the sun begin to set behind the palm trees into the ocean beyond. She sat as she had done so many times thinking of that last fight two weeks before. She remembered how Don had at first denied being with Teresa, but then when she had forced him to admit it, how he had apologized and begged her for forgiveness. She frowned a little as she thought of her harsh words, and how Don, the only man she had ever really loved, had broken down and cried like a baby when she had refused to see him again. That was two weeks ago and she had heard nothing from him since. She hadn't wanted to call him. She might want to admit that she had been unfair or to tell him how much she regretted calling him a liar; she might even say that she hadn't meant to hurt him. Then she would be a liar too. She had meant every word.

Suddenly the sound of footsteps startled her. She turned and through the gloom she thought she could make out Don's familiar figure. Was it him? Could it possibly be? The approaching figure stepped into the last patch of sunlight, and the last rays of the setting sun illuminated his dark, curly hair. He stopped, unsure of himself. "Oh, Don," she said softly, trying to control her voice. "What are you doing here?"

"Melissa," he cried. "Don't send me away."

She sighed deeply as he ran to where she sat. He took her hands tightly in his. "My darling," he whispered, "Can you ever forgive me?"

"I ...," she started but checked herself. "I guess I'm partly to blame, but..."

He interrupted her, "That's all in the past. Let's not ever talk about it again — not ever. Darling, promise me something?"

"What?" she asked cautiously.

"Here, this is for you. Please, please accept it, and wear it forever." He drew a small leather box from his pocket and leaned forward to give it to her. Suddenly the box fell from his grasp. He bent to pick it up and at that moment his glasses slipped from his nose.

"Damn! Now where have they gone? I can't see a thing without them," he explained. Melissa leaned over the arm of her chair to help him. There was a crunch as his foot crushed the glasses. "Oh, no, now I've stepped on them!" he exclaimed. "Why can't I do anything right? Why do I always ruin everything?"

Her laughter pealed around the pool. "Oh, Don you are incredible. Who could hate somebody like you? I might even love you. Come here."

Exercise

Here are some notes about what happened on page 32 of *Trust the Heart*, when Melissa and Don met for the first time at a party. Read the notes and construct their conversation.

Pat Blaze introduced her to Don.
"Oh, Melissa, I'd like you to meet Don Wainwright."

Continue:
1. They greeted each other.
2. He offered to get her a plate of food.
3. She thanked him, and asked him to get her just a little green salad.
4. He brought her a plate heaped with ham, roast beef, and potato salad and explained that the meat looked more appetizing.
5. She explained that she was a vegetarian and was on a diet, but that anyway she wasn't very hungry.
6. He asked her if she would like to dance, and she accepted.
7. He said how much he liked the music, and she agreed.
8. He complimented her on her dress, and she thanked him, and told him what a good dancer he was.
9. She invited him to watch the sunset from the terrace, and he accepted.
10. He asked if she'd like to have dinner with him the next evening, and she agreed.
11. He suggested "The Ranch Steak House" and explained that the owner was an old school friend.
12. She reminded him that she was a vegetarian and suggested "The Garden of Eden" instead.
13. He promised to pick her up at eight o'clock. She explained she liked to drive and would prefer to meet him there.

WEDDINGS

Listen to two people talking about their weddings.
Allen had a traditional church wedding. Ann was married by a Justice of the Peace.

Compare their weddings with customs and traditions in your country/region/state/city.
Tell the story of the wedding in the pictures.

Unit 78

ENGLISH
IN THE USA AND THE WORLD

History

The first census of the United States, taken in 1790, showed that 90% of the four million inhabitants were descendants of English colonists. They, therefore, spoke the language of England, which takes its name from the Anglo-Saxons, who arrived in the Celtic-speaking British Isles from northern Europe between the fourth and seventh centuries A.D. The Anglo-Saxons spoke a Germanic language which forms the basis for modern English. It was modified by the arrival of two other groups. Norse-speaking Vikings from Scandinavia came between the eighth and eleventh centuries, and their Norse language, related to Anglo-Saxon, enriched English vocabulary. Then, in 1066, French-speaking Normans conquered England. For the next three hundred years three languages co-existed. The aristocracy spoke French, the ordinary people spoke English, while Latin was used in the Church. The English that came to the American colonies in the seventeenth century had evolved from the mingling of these three tongues.

Some derived words:

Old English	*shirt, life, death, love*
Old Norse	*birth, window, ugly*
French	*boil, roast, beef, pork*
Latin	*index, item, major*

Even by 1720, however, some English colonists in America had begun to notice that their English was different. This was the natural result of an unconscious process. They had coined new words and borrowed others from the Indians, Dutch, French, and Spanish who lived in America with them. Most of these coinages and borrowings were for things which had no English equivalents since they were not encountered in England. Because of their isolation from the mother country, the colonists continued to use words that had become obsolete in England and to develop pronunciations and usages that were different from those that developed over time in England.

Some early Americanisms:

Coinages	*lightning rod, ground hog, belittle, seaboard*
New usages	*loan* (verb), *spell* (time), *card* (jokester)
Obsolete in England	*guess* (think), *fall* (autumn), *gotten* (got).
Borrowings	*moccasin, totem* (Indian), *canyon, ranch* (Spanish), *tomato, potato* (Indian via Spanish), *depot, sashay, levee* (French), *boss* (Dutch)

Political independence from England accelerated and institutionalized these differences. As the U.S. moved westward more Indian and Spanish words were added. From such groups as German and Italian immigrants and African slaves, words and intonations were borrowed and incorporated into American English. In recent decades, however, modern technologies seem to be bringing the two "Englishes" closer together again.

Features of the English Language

English has changed very much in the last 1500 years. Old English, like modern German, was a highly inflected language, i.e. most words changed their endings or forms to show their relationship to other words in the sentence according to number (singular, plural), gender (masculine, feminine, neuter), case (subject, object), tense (past, future) etc. Some modern English words still inflect, but much less so than in other European languages. The English verb "to ride" inflects into five forms (ride, rides, riding, rode, ridden), whereas the equivalent German verb has sixteen forms. The English word "the" has only one form, whereas other European languages would have several different forms. The trend towards simplicity of form is considered to be a strength of English. Another strength is the flexibility of function of individual words. Look at these uses of the word "down":

He ran for a first *down*. (noun)

He's feeling *down* today. (adjective)

The winds *downed* power lines. (verb)

She looked *down* the switch. (adverb)

They bought the brick house *down* the street. (preposition)

This flexibility, together with a flexibility towards the assimilation of words borrowed from other languages and the spontaneous creation of new words have made English what it is today, an effective medium of international communication. English has achieved this in spite of the difficulties caused by written English, which is not systematically phonetic.

Some more borrowings:

Arabic	*admiral, algebra, mattress*
Italian	*piano, violin, spaghetti*
German	*kindergarten, check* (bill), *cookbook, dumb, hold on!*
Yiddish	*bagel, chutzpah, schmaltz*
African languages	*banana, banjo, gumbo, juke box, okra, tote, yam*
Classical Greek	*theater, astronomy*
Turkish	*yogurt, kiosk*
Japanese	*tycoon, karate*
Gaelic	*whiskey*
Chinese	*tea, silk*
Portuguese	*marmalade*
Eskimo	*kayak, igloo*

Some created words:

xerox®, to xerox, xeroxed, xeroxing, sandwich, submarine, helicopter, pop, rock'n'roll, x-ray, astronaut, hot dog, telephone

English Today

Approximately 350 million people speak English as their first language. About the same number use it as a second language. It is an official language in 44 countries. In many others it is the language of business, commerce, and technology. There are many varieties of English, but Texan, Scottish, Australian, Indian, and Jamaican speakers of English, in spite of the differences in pronunciation, structure, and vocabulary, would recognize that they are all speaking the same basic language.

DEPARTURES

Yoshiko Kyo has been studying English at a college in California. She'll finish the course at the end of this week. She's going back home on Saturday. She's at a travel agency now.

Travel agent: Have a seat, please, and I'll be with you in a minute.... O.K. What can I do for you today?

Yoshiko: I want to fly to Tokyo. Are there any seats available on Saturday?

Travel agent: Just a second. Let me check.... Tokyo. What time of day did you want to go?

Yoshiko: Well, I'd rather take a non-stop flight. Is there a non-stop early in the afternoon?

Travel agent: Let's see.... JAL's 1:00 P.M. flight is full, but there's space on Pan Am's flight at the same time. The only other non-stop is China Airlines an hour later.

Yoshiko: The Pan Am flight sounds O.K. What time does it get in?

Travel agent: At 3:40 Sunday afternoon. You know all about crossing the International Date Line, of course.

Yoshiko: Yes. O.K. That'll be fine. I want to pay in cash, but I'll have to go to the bank.

Travel agent: That's all right. I'll hold the reservation for you.

Streamline Taxis: Streamline Taxi Service.

Yoshiko: I'd like to get a cab for Saturday morning please.

Streamline Taxis: Where are you going?

Yoshiko: San Francisco International Airport. There'll be three of us. How much will it be?

Streamline Taxis: We charge $45 for that trip.

Yoshiko: $45! Each?

Streamline Taxis: That's all together. What time do you want to leave?

Yoshiko: The check-in time is 12 noon, but I don't know how long it takes to get there.

Streamline Taxis: Well, we'd better pick you up at eleven, just in case traffic is heavy. Let me have your name and address.

Yoshiko: Yes, O.K. The first name is

Yoshiko—that's Y-O-S-H-I-K-O—and the last name's Kyo—K-Y-O. I'm at 128 Cortland Avenue.

Streamline Taxis: 128 Cortland Avenue. O.K. Eleven o'clock Saturday morning. Thank you.

Mr. Berman: Come in.

Yoshiko: Hi, Mr. Berman. Do you have a minute?

Mr. Berman: Sure, Yoshiko. What can I do for you?

Yoshiko: I just stopped in to say good-bye.

Mr. Berman: Oh, I see. Going back to Japan. When?

Yoshiko: I have a flight tomorrow. I'll be back at work on Monday morning.

Mr. Berman: Well, it's been nice having you here, Yoshiko.

Yoshiko: Thank you, Mr. Berman. Well—uh—I just wanted to thank you and all the other teachers.

Mr. Berman: We've all enjoyed having you as a student.

Yoshiko: I've really learned a lot. I hope to come back next year—on vacation.

Mr. Berman: Send us a postcard and let us know how you're doing, and come see us if you do get back.

Yoshiko: I'll do that.

Mr. Berman: Oh. There's the bell. Bye, Yoshiko. Have a good trip.

Yoshiko: Bye, Mr. Berman, and thanks for everything.

Yoshiko: Carlos! I'm glad I didn't miss you.

Carlos: Hi, Yoshiko. When are you leaving?

Yoshiko: Tomorrow around noon. I guess I won't see you again, so good-bye. It's been great knowing you.

Carlos: That sounds so final. Let's keep in touch, O.K.?

Yoshiko: Oh, sure. You have my address, don't you?

Carlos: Yeah, and remember, if you're ever in Caracas, look me up. I'd love to see you again.

Yoshiko: Oh, I will. You can count on that. And you do the same if you're ever in Tokyo.

Carlos: Sure. Well ... good-bye then.

Yoshiko: Bye, Carlos. You take care.

Mrs. Simmons: Yoshiko! The taxi's here. Are you ready? Do you have everything?

Yoshiko: Yes, thank you, Mrs. Simmons. And ... thank you again.

Mrs. Simmons: Thank you, Yoshiko, for the pretty plant. Now don't forget to write as soon as you get home—just to let us know that you got there safe and sound.

Yoshiko: I'll do better than that: I'll call you when the long distance rates are low tomorrow. The time difference is a mess, but I'll try not to wake you up in the middle of the night.

Mrs. Simmons: You're so sweet, Yoshiko. Good-bye now. You'd better not keep the taxi waiting. Have a nice trip. Bye.

Yoshiko: Bye. Take care of yourself. Say good-bye to Mr. Simmons for me.... Bye!

Unit 80

APPENDIX

Material recorded on cassette but not included in the text of the units is printed below.

Unit 1

1. Streamline Air Flight 604 departing at 2:45 for Kennedy Airport in New York City is now boarding at Gate 3. Passengers with tickets on Streamline 604 at 2:45 to New York Kennedy please check in at Gate 3.
2. This is the last call for Peoplexpress Flight 373 departing at 2:30 for Houston. Passengers on Peoplexpress 373 at 2:30 to Houston should board now at Gate 1.
3. Continental Airlines announces that Flight 127 to Houston and El Paso is delayed. Continental's Flight 127 to Houston and El Paso is now scheduled to depart at 3:00 from Gate 7. Passengers on Continental 127 are advised that their flight will depart from Gate 7 at 3:00.
4. Peoplexpress announces that Flight 881 to New York City's La Guardia Airport at 2:55 will depart from Gate 2 and will start boarding in 10 minutes. At this time will passengers who need special help in boarding please go to Gate 2 for Peoplexpress 881 to New York La Guardia at 2:55.
5. Streamline Air Flight 403 to Atlanta with connections to Miami and other points south will depart on schedule at 3:05 from Gate 4. We repeat: Streamline Air 403 will depart as scheduled at 3:05 for Atlanta. Passengers should make their seat selection at Gate 4 prior to boarding which will begin in 5 minutes.

Unit 13

A. Airport announcements
1. This is the last call for flight 932 for Syracuse, now boarding at Gate 14. Scheduled departure time is 3:25.
2. Flight 217 with nonstop service to Caracas is boarding at Gate 34. The flight is 10 minutes behind schedule and will depart at 3:40.
3. Flight 558 with service to Hartford, Connecticut and Springfield, Massachusetts is now ready for boarding at Gate 26. The flight will depart on schedule at 3:45.
4. Pan Am's flight 563 to Detroit is now pre-boarding. Passengers with small children or who require special help in boarding should go now to Gate 12. The flight will leave as scheduled at 4:30.
5. Will Pan Am passenger Rita Chambers holding a ticket on flight 67, scheduled to depart for San Francisco at 4:30, please go to Gate 32 for a new seat assignment prior to boarding. Ms. Rita Chambers.
6. Passengers for Los Angeles, may I please have your attention. Pan Am's nonstop service to Los Angeles, Flight 811 scheduled to depart at 4:30 has been delayed due to late arrival from London. Flight 811 will now depart at 4:50 from Gate 30. Boarding will begin in 15 minutes.

B. In-flight announcements
1. Good afternoon, ladies and gentlemen. This is your captain, Tom Brown. We'd like to welcome you aboard flight 811 and to apologize for the delay. We had some bumpy weather over the Atlantic and arrived late from London. Now we are experiencing another slight delay as we wait for clearance from Air Traffic Control. We don't expect it will be more than five minutes, and we hope to arrive in Los Angeles at about 7:30 local time.
2. This is the captain again. I just wanted to apologize

again for the delays and to let you know that we are almost back on schedule. Our Boeing 767 is cruising at an altitude of about 30,000 feet at an airspeed of 560 miles per hour. We are above the state of Maryland and that's Washington, D.C. over to the left of the plane. The temperature in Los Angeles is 79° Fahrenheit (that's 26° Celsius). The day is clear and sunny—really unusual for Los Angeles. We ask that while you are in your seats you keep your seat belts fastened in case we hit some unexpected turbulence.
3. We're beginning our approach now to Los Angeles International Airport. Please make sure your seat belt is securely fastened, return your seat and tray to their original upright position, and extinguish all smoking materials. No smoking is allowed until you are in the airport terminal building.
4. We hope you have had a pleasant and enjoyable flight and we'd like to thank you for flying Pan Am today. Please remain in your seat until the plane has come to a complete and final stop at the gate. If you have any questions about connecting flights, please see the Pan Am agents who will meet our flight.

Unit 15

Bargaining
Sally: Excuse me. How much do you want for this bowl?
Stand Owner: Let's see.... Hmm ... That's an outstanding piece of Depression glass—in perfect shape. It's worth eighty bucks.
Sally: Eighty dollars! Oh, I couldn't possibly pay that much. It's a shame. It really is nice.
Stand Owner: I said it was *worth* eighty bucks. I'm only asking sixty.
Sally: Sixty dollars?
Stand Owner: Yeah, it's a real bargain.
Sally: Oh, I'm sure it is. But I can't afford that.
Stand Owner: Well, look. Tell you what I'll do. I'll make it fifty-five. I can't go any lower than that.
Sally: I'll give you thirty-five.
Stand Owner: Thirty-five! Come on, lady. You've got to be kidding. I paid more than that for it myself. Take it for fifty. It's worth every penny.
Sally: Well, maybe I could give you forty.
Stand Owner: Forty-eight. That's my final price.
Sally: Forty-five.
Stand Owner: Make it forty-seven.
Sally: O.K. Forty-seven.
Stand Owner: Let me wrap it up for you. There you are, lady—a real bargain!
Sally: Yeah, thanks a lot.

Unit 44

1
Our five finalists are Miss Florida, Rita Rae Simpson; Miss New York, LaDonna Lincoln; Miss Minnesota, Amy Lou Peterson; Miss Wyoming, Lucia Delgado; and Miss Arkansas, Susan Lee Jamison. Now watch the screen and listen to the interviews conducted by the judges at the beginning of the week.

2
Judge: So you're Rita Mae Simpson from Tampa, Florida.
Rita Rae: That's "Rita Rae," not "Mae."
Judge: Oh, excuse me, Rita Rae. You're a student at the University of Miami, aren't you?

Rita Rae: Yes, I'm going to be an elementary school teacher.
Judge: How old are you, Rita Rae?
Rita Rae: I'll be 19 next December.
Judge: What do you like to do in your spare time?
Rita Rae: Well, I like sewing.
Judge: That's a beautiful dress you're wearing. Did you make it?
Rita Rae: Yes, with a little help from my mother. I also like cooking. I do most of the cooking for my family when I'm home.
Judge: What's your greatest ambition, Rita Rae?
Rita Rae: I love children. I really want to work with children. I learn so much from them.
Judge: I see. And if you could have one wish, what would it be?
Rita Rae: I'd wish for a large family.
Judge: Thank you, Rita Rae.

3
Judge: Now you're LaDonna Lincoln from New Rochelle, New York. How old are you, LaDonna?
LaDonna: I'm 20 today.
Judge: Well, happy birthday!
LaDonna: Thank you. It's such fun to be here on my birthday.
Judge: I'm sure it is. Tell me, LaDonna, where do you go to school?
LaDonna: I'm in my junior year at Syracuse University. I'm studying drama and singing because my ambition is to be an actress.
Judge: That's interesting. And what about your hobbies?
LaDonna: Well, I love playing the piano. And when I have some spare time, I go sailing.
Judge: What about one wish?
LaDonna: Oh, that's easy. I've really thought about it. I would wish for world peace. It's the most important thing in the world. Don't you think so?
Judge: It certainly is important. Thank you, LaDonna.

4
Judge: Here we have Amy Lou Peterson from Minneapolis, Minnesota. How are you, Amy Lou?
Amy: I'm fine, thank you. And it's "Amy," not "Amy Lou."
Judge: O.K., Amy. How old are you?
Amy: I'm 21. I'm in my last year at the University of Minnesota.
Judge: What are you studying there?
Amy: I'm majoring in physics.
Judge: What's your ambition, Amy?
Amy: Well, when I finish graduate school in a few years, I want to become an astronaut.
Judge: An astronaut? That's wonderful! What about your hobbies?
Amy: Well, I love astronomy, of course. I also like horseback riding. I go whenever I can.
Judge: And what about a wish?
Amy: I'd wish for happiness for everyone.
Judge: Thank you, Amy. It has been interesting talking to you.

5
Judge: And you're Lucia Delgado from Cheyenne, Wyoming. How old are you, Lucia?
Lucia: I'm 18.
Judge: I know you're a student at the University of Wyoming, and you're studying law.
Lucia: Well, yes and no. I *am* studying at the University of Wyoming, but I've changed my major re-

cently. I'm now majoring in sociology. You see, my ambition is ... well, it's to be a police officer. So when I graduate, I'm going to the Police Academy.

Judge: That's wonderful! And what do you do in your spare time?

Lucia: Well, I like judo. I like photography, but I'm not very good yet.

Judge: What would you wish for if you could wish for anything in the world?

Lucia: I'd definitely wish for good health—for everyone.

Judge: Thank you, Lucia.

6

Judge: And here is 21-year old Susan Lee Jamison from the University of Arkansas. Is that right, Susan?

Susan: Yes, but I'm a high fashion model in my spare time. I don't have much time for studying.

Judge: I see. What abut your hobbies, Susan?

Susan: I like reading and swimming, although I don't have much time to do either. I'm so busy.

Judge: Uh, well, Susan, what about your ambition?

Susan: My ambition is very clear. I want to be Miss Universe.

Judge: And if you could wish for anything, what would it be?

Susan: Let me see ... I would wish for ... it would be ... uh ... probably ... good luck. Yes, good luck. I'll need it.

Judge: Thank you, Susan.

7

Ron Parks: The judges have just handed me the envelope with the results of our Miss America Beauty Contest. I'm going to read the results in reverse order. Fourth runner-up and winner of a $5,000 scholarship is Miss Arkansas, Susan Lee Jamison. Third runner-up and winner of a 7,000 scholarship is Miss Florida, Rita Rae Simpson. Second runner-up and winner of a $10,000 scholarship is Miss Minnesota, Amy Lou Peterson. First runner-up and winner of a $15,000 scholarship is ... Miss Wyoming, Lucia Delgado. The new Miss America is LaDonna Lincoln, Miss New York, winner of a $25,000 scholarship. Congratulations, LaDonna.

Unit 52

Donna

Well, she's really talkative and funny. She's about—well, in her late teens. She's pretty tall with a really good figure. She has a kind of oval-shaped face, and a turned up nose—very pretty in a way. She has long wavy black hair and—uh—blue eyes with very long eyelashes. Her complexion is—well, she's olive skinned. Her lips are very full, and she has dimples—the cutest little dimples in her cheeks.

Chuck

He's a real big guy, you know, well-built with very broad shoulders. Not fat at all, but, solid. He's in his early thirties. He's dark-skinned, and he has a long face with thin lips. Oh, and a scar on his chin. He has dark curly hair, almost black, and wears it short but with long sideburns and a mustache. His eyes—I haven't really noticed the color—he wears glasses—brown, I guess. He has thick eyebrows and a kind of a long straight nose. He's pretty reserved and quiet, sometimes even moody.

Janet

She's very sophisticated. Well-dressed, one of those expensive haircuts, you know. I'd say she was in her late thirties or early forties, but she looks younger. She's about average height and very slim. Her hair's very blonde—dyed, I think, but I'm not sure. It's always very neat, not long. She has light gray eyes with thin eyebrows. Her face is always suntanned and very well made up. It's an attractive face—not really beautiful,

but attractive—handsome, if you know what I mean. High cheekbones, small chin—oh, and there's a beauty mark on her left cheek. She's a very confident and reliable sort of person, very sociable and always very, very polite.

Bob

Bob's a terrific person. He's elderly but not really old—cheerful and friendly and funny. He's probably in his early seventies. He has white hair, receding a little, and a small white beard. He's medium build, a little bit overweight maybe. He has nice, big brown eyes, and he always seems to be smiling—lots of wrinkles around the eyes, but they're smile lines not frown lines. He has a very high, lined forehead that makes him look very intelligent—which he is, of course.

Unit 65

Craig Williams: Hello, doctor.

Dr. Casey: Hello, Mr. Williams. What brings you here today?

Craig: I'm not sure, doctor, but I haven't been feeling too well. I think I might have the flu.

Dr. Casey: Uh huh. There's a lot of it going around these days. Tell me how you've been feeling.

Craig: Well, very tired, and I'm aching all over. I've been sneezing a lot and feeling pretty feverish, hot and cold all the time. Oh, and I've had a sore throat.

Dr. Casey: Any vomiting?

Craig: No, but I don't feel very hungry. I just have no appetite at all.

Dr. Casey: Well, let me take a look at you. Come sit up here. Now, open your mouth and say, "Ahh." Uh huh. Your throat's a little inflamed, and I see the glands in your neck are swollen. Unbutton your shirt and let me listen to your chest. Breathe deeply. Hmm. I'm going to check your temperature. Don't talk for a minute; just keep the thermometer under your tongue. I'll write out a prescription for you, but you know that the best thing is rest. Go to bed and drink lots of liquids. If you have a fever, take 2 aspirin every four hours. Come in again if you're not better in 3 or 4 days.

Unit 72

Real Estate Agent: I'm afraid it hasn't been kept up very well. The man who lived here was in his eighties when he died a few months ago. His daughter doesn't want the place, so she's selling it.

Robin: I can see why. It looks as though it needs a lot of work done on it.

Agent: True, but the price is very reasonable. It could be a great do-it-yourself project.

Gene: Hm! I'm not that good with my hands. We'd have to get most of the work done for us, wouldn't we, Robin?

Robin: Oh, I don't know. Let's look at the inside.

Agent: Oh, sure. Let's go in through the kitchen door.

Robin: Whew! Look at that sink. It must have been there since the house was built.

Gene: It's big, though, and plenty of light. We always wanted an eat-in kitchen. We'd have to have all new kitchen units and the major appliances—new stove, refrigerator, dishwasher, garbage disposal.

Robin: Well, we'd have to start with having new plumbing installed for a modern kitchen. And we'd have to do something about this floor. I guess we could put down vinyl tiles ourselves.

Gene: Yeah, you're right. Is that the only electrical outlet there?

Agent: I'm afraid it is.

Gene: It looks pretty old. I'm sure the whole place would need rewiring. We'd certainly have to have that done even before the plumbing. We would need a lot more outlets too.

Agent: Would you like to see the rest of the house? The dining room and living room are through here.

Robin: Oh, wow! These walls! I guess we'd have to cover all the walls with sheet rock.

Gene: That's easier said than done. We'd have to get somebody to put up the sheet rock; then we could do the painting. And, of course, the ceilings need painting, but we could do that too. What's the upstairs like?

Agent: More of the same. As you say all the walls and ceilings need work, but look at these floors. They're beautiful, aren't they? Now, as you know, there's no bathroom.

Robin: Yes, I noticed the bathtub in the kitchen. What about the toilet?

Agent: That's the little outhouse in back. Anyway, I was about to say that you could have the small bedroom upstairs converted into a bathroom.

Gene: More plumbing costs, but of course we'd have to have it done. We couldn't live without indoor plumbing.

Robin: Absolutely. Is there anything else that has to be done?

Agent: Well, you'd have to get the roof repaired pretty soon.

Robin: The sooner the better if you ask me. It looks like water has been coming in over there.

Gene: And we'd have to have a new oil burner put in, I guess. Plus, we'd have to have the windows weather-proofed to keep the heat in during the winter. Humpf! I bet it'll cost a fortune to heat this place.

Agent: Well, of course, you'd want to insulate before you have the sheet rock put on.

Gene: Yeah, I guess we could put in the insulation. So, when it comes down to it the only things we can do are put down the vinyl tiles, put in the insulation, and paint the place.

Robin: Right, and I wonder how good a job we'd do even with that. Well, thanks for showing us around, but I think we'd be better off knocking it down and starting all over again!

Unit 75

9:00

Rosa: Good morning. Peter Danieli's office.

Judy: Hi, Rosa. It's Judy. Can you give Peter a message, please? I won't be in till Friday. I have the flu. I saw the doctor this morning.

Rosa: O.K., Judy. I'll give him the message. I hope you feel better soon.

9:40

Rosa: Peter Danieli's office. May I help you?

Joe: May I speak to Mr. Danieli, please?

Rosa: I'm sorry, he's out of the office today. He'll be back tomorrow. May I take a message?

Joe: This is Joe Watkins calling. Please tell Peter that I can't make the meeting tomorrow. Something important's come up. I'll call him Wednesday morning.

11:30

Rosa: Hi, George. What can I do for you?

George: Peter isn't there, is he?

Rosa: No, not until tomorrow.

George: Well, it's just that I want Friday off. You see, my grandmother died yesterday. I'll have to go to the funeral.

Rosa: Oh, I'm sorry. How old was she?

George: 92.

12:15

Rosa: Peter Danieli's office.

Salesman: I'd like to speak to Mr. Danieli, please.

Rosa: I'm sorry, he isn't in today. Would you like to leave a message?

Salesman: Sure. I'm calling from Wilson Auto Sales. It's about his new car. Well, it isn't ready yet. There's a mix-up at the factory.

2:10

Rosa: Good afternoon, Mr. Danieli's office.

Anne: Good afternoon. This is Anne Mori from Western Video Systems. Peter's at the trade show in Chicago, isn't he?

Rosa: Yes, that's right. He should be here tomorrow.

Anne: Well, can you give him this message first thing in the morning? I'm afraid we have to cancel our last order. The customers have changed their minds again.

3:20

Rosa: Good afternoon. Mr. Danieli's office.

Juan: Hello. This is Juan Gonzalez speaking. Is Peter there?

Rosa: No, I'm afraid he's away on business today. Can I give him a message, Mr. Gonzalez?

Juan: Yes. I may be in town from the 21st to the 25th. I want to see Peter then, if it's possible. I'll call to confirm it.

4:35

Rosa: Mr. Danieli's office.

Susan: Hello. Is Mr. Danieli in?

Rosa: No, he'll be here tomorrow morning. May I take a message?

Susan: My name is Susan Ellis. Can you have him call me as soon as he gets back from Chicago? It's urgent.

4:55

Rosa: Peter Danieli's office.

Andy: Hello, Rosa. This is Andy Berra.

Rosa: Oh, hello, Mr. Berra.

Andy: I've got an important message for Peter. Please give it to him the minute he gets in tomorrow. Just say, "Don't fill any orders for Syncom Company until further notice." It's very important. I'll explain later.

Unit 78

A Church Wedding

Allen and Caroline were married recently.

"Our wedding was pretty typical, I guess. Caroline and I met about three years ago and last summer we decided to get married. We both wanted a traditional wedding. I suppose it's expensive, and some people say it's a waste of money, but it is a day to remember all your life. Anyway, we really did it to make our folks happy, and we both wanted to get married in church. Caroline's father rented a big limousine to bring her to the church—we wanted the whole works! You know—champagne, all the men in tuxedos, all the women in long dresses. My best man and the ushers rented their tuxedos, but I decided to buy mine. Caroline's maid of honor was her sister, and she had two bridesmaids—her cousins. The ring bearer was her nephew, and the flower girl was my niece. They were really too young and were very distracting during the ceremony. I wasn't in great shape that day because my bachelor party went on until five o'clock in the morning. I do remember the pictures, though. The photographer seemed to take forever to take them. Having them now makes it all worth it. We were very lucky; it was a beautiful sunny day in June. The reception was at the Carlton Hotel. It must have cost Caroline's dad a bundle. The toasts went on too long, and it took twenty minutes just to read all the telegrams. And the presents were fabulous! We danced and ate and drank champagne—very nice. When it came to the getaway, I had been very careful and parked my car around the corner, but naturally they somehow managed to find out where it was. You should have seen what they'd done to it! It was covered with paint and lipstick, and they'd tied tin cans to the back bumper, but I suppose that's a tradition. But, anyway, they didn't find out where we were spending our honeymoon. We went to Puerto Rico."

A Justice of the Peace Wedding

Ann and Stuart were married by a Justice of the Peace.

"Stu and I met last year. We were both working in New York, although Stu's from New Orleans and I'm from Providence. We didn't want a fancy wedding, and neither of us are particularly religious, so we were married by a Justice of the Peace. Another thing is that our families aren't so well off, and it seemed crazy to go to that expense when you can really use the money for other things. I mean, I was giving up my apartment, and we wanted to fix up Stu's apartment. Anyway, we just invited our folks and a couple of close friends, who were the witnesses. It was all very simple—and short. We didn't have a reception or anything. We just had a few drinks at our place. We didn't even bother with a cake. And we didn't have a honeymoon. Stu's just started his own business, and we couldn't afford to take the time."